The Right Fight

The RightFight

How to Live a Loving Life

JOHN KENNEDY VAUGHAN

BROWN
CHRISTIAN PRESS
A DIVISION OF
BROWN BOOKS PUBLISHING

The Right Fight
How to Live a Loving Life

Unless otherwise indicated, Scriptures are taken from the Holy Bible, New International Version®, NIV®. Copyright © 1973, 1978, 1984, 2011 by Biblica, Inc.™ Used by permission of Zondervan. All rights reserved worldwide, www.zondervan.com. The "NIV" and "New International Version" are trademarks registered in the United States Patent and Trademark Office by Biblica, Inc.™

Brown Christian Press
16250 Knoll Trail Drive, Suite 205
Dallas, Texas 75248
www.BrownChristianPress.com
(972) 381-0009

A New Era in Publishing®

Names: Vaughan, John Kennedy
Title: The right fight : how to live a loving life / John Kennedy Vaughan.
Description: Dallas, Texas : Brown Christian Press, a division of Brown Books
    Publishing, [2018]
Identifiers: ISBN 9781612542959 (hardcover)
Subjects: LCSH: Love--Religious aspects--Christianity. | God (Christianity)--
    Love. | Fear--Religious aspects--Christianity. | Choice (Psychology)--
    Religious aspects--Christianity. | Christian life.
Classification: LCC BV4639 .V38 2018 | DDC 241.4--dc23

ISBN 978-1-61254-295-9 (HC)
LCCN 2018951841

Printed in the United States
10 9 8 7 6 5 4 3 2 1

For more information or to contact the author, please go to
www.ShieldsOfStrength.com.

This book is dedicated to my grandfather, Ed Vaughan.
Although I never met him, his enormous influence
on my life reverberates today. His example shows
me there are no bounds to a truly selfless love.

Contents

Foreword

I thought I was only going so that I could eat lunch and give counsel, but I left chewing on some new concepts that would take a long time to digest. Looking back, it was the brief, unexpected conversation after the meeting that I would remember and wrestle with the most. It was a conversation that caused me to deconstruct and then reconstruct my conceptual framework about a subject that determines if life is going to be fruitful or fruitless. I was one of five people that was invited to the lunch meeting to offer advice to an aspiring minister. I was supposed to be the one leaving someone else with something to think about.

One by one, the five of us took turns sharing our personal experiences and serving up what we hoped to be eye-opening advice. I remember each one of my colleagues offering nuggets of wisdom, and I hoped that when it was my turn, I could do the same. But when it was Kenny's turn, he presented an insightful, literally life-changing perspective on a subject that I thought I had already figured out but knew deep down that I didn't live out. And while his insight about the subject of love exposed my self-serving definition and practice of love, it was the humility that came out during his presentation that convinced me that he not only believed what he was talking about but lived it. His content about the subject matter and the way he presented it arrested my attention, and I had to hear more than just a five-minute sound bite. As we were shaking hands and saying our goodbyes, Kenny and I engaged in a brief personal conversation in which he challenged common misconceptions about love accompanied by simple solutions that would radically transform my interaction with others. That brief conversation began a friendship that continues to this day, and it was the start of a personal journey that would help me move toward becoming a more loving husband, father, employer, leader, and friend.

What you hold in your hand is a gift that could radically change every interaction and relationship you have. I got it in bits and pieces. You get it as a whole. If you're like me, you have purchased book after book with the hope that someone else's insight would help expand your perspective and introduce you to truth that would lead to needed change. If you're like me, most of those books were quickly abandoned before chapter three because it didn't meet the "substance" or "interest" test. I'm confident that *The Right Fight* will hold your attention and challenge your perspective and application of love. And if it causes you to rethink what love is and helps you love others better, it will not only be a gift to you, but a long-remembered gift to everyone you have the opportunity to love. Can you imagine the value you would show your family and friends if you really became a loving person? Can you imagine the legacy you would leave if you really became a loving person?

—Reg Lloyd

Preface

This book was born from my desire to share with my children what I had learned about living a fruitful life. More than anything, I wanted to teach them that the quality of their lives would depend on their decisions every day to choose love, not fear—to be fearlessly loving, considering others before themselves at every turn.

This book is the result of almost a decade of work, and over the years, it has only become clearer to me how critical the lessons contained inside are to living a strong and fruitful life.

My prayer is that this book will help you to understand what fear really is, what love really is, and how they work to frame our lives. I hope, from these pages, that you can find the power and the insight to build strong roots for your life fed not by selfish fear but by selfless love. May the choices lined out on these pages set you on the path of strength and boundless hope and joy—in the hard times and the good.

Acknowledgments

Thank you, Mom and Dad. You loved me, Bonnie, and Gabe so well that God's love for us all made perfect sense. From both of you I learned that there is no end to a parent's love and that love gives and protects, expecting nothing in return.

A thanks to Mr. and Mrs. Roccaforte for loving Tammie and leading her to the truth of God's Word. Her love for me and our children is a reflection of both your hearts.

My thanks to Paul Laminack, who helped me turn an idea in my head into a picture of a live, fruitful tree fed by roots of love. And a special thanks to Marcia Davis, Julianne Webber, and Hallie Raymond for helping communicate these life-changing truths, and to the people at Brown Books for helping me get them to the world.

Most of all, thank you, Tammie, for loving me and leading me from fear to love. You're the most loving woman I know, and somehow, thanks be to God, I get to be your husband. I have seen more courage in you then any man I have ever known, and your constant clarity on the source of your strength brought me to Jesus. Thank you for believing in me when I didn't think I could and for leading me to He Who helps me do all things. Without you and Jesus, I am nothing.

CHAPTER ONE

Ice Cream, My Kids, and My New Truck

"No more ice-cream runs," I said to the kids. I was not trying to be mean, but it was really the only responsible thing to do.

My three kids—Faith, Grace, and Kennedy—were nine, six, and two at the time. My wife, Tammie, and I have always liked to do little things with them now and then that are simple but fun and kind of spontaneous. As a result, you never know when a do-nothing evening might turn into a 9 p.m. ice-cream, taco, or french-fry run. My mom used to make similar trips with me and my siblings, and I still remember the excitement of those nighttime excursions. I love sharing those simple adventures with my children, seeing their excitement, and knowing we are making special memories.

But with three kids, it was inevitable that every single ice-cream run would end up with a mess in my truck. Let's face it: a child under the age of ten has a one-in-three chance of spilling their ice cream in the vehicle. I had three children under the age of ten, so our chances of a spill were mathematically guaranteed. That was frustrating for me, but before, my truck had been old anyway, so I had thought, *What the heck!* It was family fun. So, after an ice-cream run and the inevitable spills, I would scrub the messes out of the carpet as much as I could. The extra work was worth it. I happily paid the price.

Now I had a new truck. Now evening food runs and the inevitable spills were going to come at a higher price for me. As I had begun to weigh the cost, it had occurred to me that I might set a bad example for my children if I didn't take the best possible care of something as nice as my shiny new truck. Plus, I just plain didn't want any ice-cream spills in my new truck. I didn't even want any dust in it.

The only reasonable solution was to stop the ice-cream runs. I knew I needed to announce the new rule immediately. I didn't want to deal with the drama that would come the next evening at 9 p.m. when someone yelled out, "Ice-cream run!" and I had to say, "Negative. No way. Forget it. Not in my new truck." Of course, the new rule banning ice-cream runs didn't go over well, but the kids saw my character-istic "I'm-not-budging-on-this" look in my eye when I made the announcement, so it was disappointing but done with. The next night, when the call for an ice-cream run rang out, Faith brought everyone back down to reality when she responded, "Remember, we can't. Dad's new truck."

It was easier for me to stick with the new rule the first few times I had to remind everyone that the ice-cream runs were history, but a few weeks into the deal, I started feeling selfish. I began chewing on the truth: I was taking something from my kids and my family that I liked sharing with them, all because I was afraid of the mess that it might make. So, I started thinking of ways to resume our ice-cream runs without sacrificing the cleanliness of my new truck.

My first idea was that Tammie could drive, and I would supervise the kids. The problem with this idea was that kids are so creative in the ways they spill ice cream. I knew that I could have an army in the back seat, and the spills would happen anyway, in ways no one had even imagined. After a great deal of thought, the only solution I could think of was to put towels down on the floor and in the seats, put the kids in the seats, put towels in their laps, and then caution them about being careful. So, that's what we did.

I thought I had it all figured out. The next night, I said the magic words: "Hey, how about an ice-cream run?"

The kids looked at me, at each other, then back at me, and asked together, "What about your truck, Dad?"

I told them I was sorry for being selfish, that I had thought about everything and had come up with a good idea. We could use towels to protect the truck. Then I talked with them about being careful when eating the ice cream.

I put the towels down on the floorboards and on the seats, put the kids in the seats, and then put the towels in the kids' laps, and off we went.

Much to my surprise, the actual trip was spill-free. I could hardly believe it. As I pulled into the driveway back at home, I was thinking the whole problem all this time had been that I had never emphasized enough how to be careful when eating ice cream in the truck.

I hit the garage door opener, pulled into the garage, and put the truck in park. That's when it all came undone. Suddenly, big blobs of melting ice cream came flying at me from the back seat, sticky globs of goop sailing through the air between the two front bucket seats in a clear path to the dash. My first thought was that the kids had actually thrown it! I must have turned as red as a beet, and, like an angry lion ready to pounce, I turned around to confront the kids in the back seat. I saw that Faith was in her seat holding her and Kennedy's empty cups. The expression on her face was telling me, "It wasn't me, Daddy. I promise." Kennedy was already out of his seat and on the floor, and Grace was holding an empty cup out in front of her with a look on her face

3

that said, "Dad, I promise I didn't mean to." Her face looked like she was peering into the eyes of the Grim Reaper.

I was about to let Grace have it for being so irresponsible, so careless, so inconsiderate, so selfish—and then I would go on to explain how we would never have another ice-cream run again. I turned my head back toward the dash to check the damage to the truck, and that's when I noticed the ice cream on the dash was melting and running into the cracks around the buttons on my radio. I remembered my last truck had had the same thing happen, and for ten years I had fought with a sticky dash button. If I pushed that button, it might pop back out, or it might stick down, so I would have to hit it over and over to get it to release. Now my new truck was about to have sticky buttons. I didn't know what to do, but I knew I didn't want this. All I could think of was to get that melting ice cream out from behind the radio buttons as quickly as possible, and the only way I could think to do that was to start sucking it out.

I'm a little embarrassed to say that's just what I did. I wrapped my lips around the buttons and started sucking with all my might. It worked, too! I sucked all that ice cream out. This time, there would be no sticky buttons! Poor Tammie and Faith were looking at me as if I'd lost my mind. Grace looked more scared than ever because now Dad was trying to eat his radio. No one knew what to expect next, especially me. Though Tammie didn't say anything, she looked like she wanted to ask me, "What the heck are you doing?"

The truth is that, at first, I didn't realize what I was doing. My immediate reactions to the spill were anger, selfish pride, and fear over what the spill would cost me in messing up the truck. The truth is that I was about to chip away at the self-esteem and trust of my children. I was about to model the poorest example of love and self-control for them, and I was about to compromise our relationship and our memories over a little ice cream that had accidentally spilled in my new truck.

I am thankful for the distraction of the dash buttons getting pelted with ice cream, because that distraction gave me time for a reality check. Once I had eliminated, to my satisfaction, the dangers of driving another decade fighting with sticky dash buttons, I took a breath and struggled for a rational thought—and it was a struggle. Then everything hit me like a ton of bricks. I was reminded of the lessons I had learned through the years about love and fear: from God's word, from Tammie, from fifteen years of chasing the dream of winning a national championship as an athlete, and from my mom and dad and family.

Fear always protects itself without regard for the truth or others. Love always defends the truth and others without regard for itself. I remembered that saying something hurtful could only take a moment, but the weight of those words could last a lifetime. I recalled how love always seeks the truth, but the truth is almost always hidden. I remembered that the only person I could ever lovingly sacrifice was myself.

People will forget what you say, and they may even forget what you do, but they seldom forget how you make them feel. It is extremely difficult to live lovingly, but it is easy to recognize a loving sacrifice when we see it. I wanted my kids to enjoy ice-cream runs and, as adults, be able to look back and cherish the memories of those times. I realized I was about to sacrifice all that for my truck and that I was acting and reacting as if I had never learned anything at all. I was letting fear push love right out the truck window.

For me, that night's cup of ice cream was tasting bittersweet, turning sourer by the minute as I considered the truth. I knew that I would burn that truck every day for the rest of my life before I would purposely hurt my kids, my precious Grace, Faith, and Kennedy. I thought about how sensitive Grace is. She is a very special young lady. She gives her very best and all her heart to everything she does, just like Faith and Kennedy and their mom, but Grace feels and gives times ten. Even when I gently tell Grace she has made a mistake, she will hide under her bed and cry for half an hour. Grace would have never thrown that ice cream, but I had been about to treat her as if she had thrown it just to mess up my truck.

I paused again, tried to compose myself, and choked down the frustration I felt before I turned back around to ask, "Grace, what happened?"

Grace still looked like she was seeing a ghost. Despite my attempt to control my expression, I could tell the anger on my face was still visible to her and everyone else in the truck. Grace answered, "Daddy, I promise I did everything you said. I was really careful. I kept the towel in my lap and everything. I was being so careful getting out of the seat and holding the cup out in front of me, but Kennedy did what you always taught him. You know, Dad, how he rolls forward to get out of his car seat and does the front flip onto the floor. When he flipped, his heel hit my cup, and that's why the ice cream went flying. I'm so sorry, Daddy. I promise I didn't mean to."

I paused for a minute to consider that Kennedy was acting like a two-year-old because that's exactly what he was and that he really had done what I taught him to do. Grace had done all she could and more to avoid a spill, and circumstances had just led to the ice cream flying through my truck.

I saw before me a choice: I could sacrifice the cleanliness of my truck and continue the ice-cream runs with my family, which would be the loving thing to do, or I could scream at Grace, act unlovingly toward my family, and take the ice-cream runs away again, which would be the selfish thing to do. In the end, the choice was clear. I would sacrifice my truck rather than my family any day.

The funny thing is that my decision cost me something then but continues to benefit me and my family to this day. We had another talk about no more flipping out of the car seat when ice cream or drinks were present, and we have enjoyed those ice-cream runs ever since. I still keep towels on the floor of my truck twenty-four seven. I bought some black towels to match the interior of my truck, along with a few extras, so I can switch them out when the ones in the truck get dirty. It's been a few years now, and my truck carpet still looks new, even though I only see that carpet when I pick up the towels.

On a more serious note, the lessons running through my head that evening were a great example of the journey I had been on for years to figure out exactly what love is, how it works, and what its enemies are. I wanted to identify the things that determine whether love or fear rules my life. I was starting to realize that love was the most basic fundamental of a strong life and that if I wanted to live a strong life for my family, my friends, and my God, I had better figure out exactly what love was, how it worked, and how to make sure it ruled my life.

Chapter Two

Strong Foundations

If we are to learn anything, we have to start with the basics. I learned the incredible importance of fundamentals chasing my lifelong dream of winning a US water skiing national championship. I had received a rare opportunity to train for a week with Jay Bennett, the USA team coach, considered by many to be the greatest ski-jumping coach in the world. Skiers came from all over the world to train with Jay Bennett. I had high expectations and couldn't wait for him to see me jump. I hoped that he would be impressed. I was ready to learn, and I couldn't wait to have a chance to see the revolutionary techniques and skills that separated the greatest athletes in our sport from the rest of the crowd.

After unloading my luggage into my bunk room, I wasted no time grabbing my gear and heading to the starting dock, where all the skiers were waiting for their turns to ski with Jay's coaching. While waiting, I watched the world's greatest jumpers from different nations taking their turns. Some had translators because they didn't know the English language. It was amazing to see so many great skiers in one place, and I listened to everything Jay said to each skier. Most of the jumpers were of the caliber I hoped I would soon become, and I wanted to learn everything I could from them. I wanted to know the secrets most skiers didn't know that could help me break through to the top level of our sport. When my turn came to ski, Jay smiled and said, "Kenny, how have you been skiing?"

I said, "Jay, I'm skiing well, and jumping farther than ever, but still not where I need to be."

Jay said, "Well, let's see why—and by the way, you won't need your helmet. I just want to see you ski before we hit the ramp."

I thought that was a little strange, especially since I was the only jumper he asked to leave his helmet on the dock. It was also a little embarrassing since all the other jumpers were close enough to hear Jay. I couldn't wait for everyone to see me jump, and now I had to simply ski, but I shook it off and thought, *It's OK. Jay knows what he's doing, and he's taught some of the best jumpers in the world for years.* So, I left the dock and decided I would just ride my skis as if I were jumping but not jump. I figured if I were just going to ride them, I would ride them like a champ. I felt I was probably pushing seventy miles per hour crossing behind the boat as if I would be headed right into the ramp. I felt in control and balanced, but at the end of the lake, Jay asked the boat driver to stop the boat. I sank into the water, and the boat idled back until I was sitting in the water in my wetsuit with all my gear but no helmet. My first thought was that Jay was going to tell me he was so pleased with my skiing that he wanted me to take a jump, and I was thinking to myself, *I wonder if he remembers I will need my helmet?* I was so excited to jump that I was willing to jump without a helmet. I grew up jumping without one anyway. Then Jay said, "Kenny, you don't even know how to ski properly."

I responded, "Jay, let me show you how I jump."

He said, "Until you learn how to ski, you won't jump on my site." Then he pointed to a nineteen-year-old boy sitting next to him in the boat. He was an intern learning how to coach skiing under Jay's mentorship. Jay said the boy would be working with me over the next few days to teach me how to ski properly. He said that after I had mastered skiing, I could take a few singles (a term used to describe low-speed beginner jumps).

A thousand thoughts went through my mind. First I thought, *You have no idea what you're talking about!* At the same time, I was embarrassed that he'd just said all that in front of the boat driver and this kid that I could ski circles around. *It's not fair; no one even let me jump, and I came all this way so excited to train with Jay. Now I'm supposed to ski with this kid no one even knows, so he can teach me what I learned fifteen years ago at the age of nine.* I hadn't been on the site more than a few hours, and I felt humiliated, shamed, overlooked, left out, and like a total fool. What I wanted to do more than anything was pack up all my gear and leave. I was in a fog of disbelief, but I knew I only had two choices: leave, or totally humble myself. All my feelings screamed at me to leave, but I had waited all my life for this opportunity. I knew Jay was not a fool. I had seen many good jumpers become great with his coaching, and if I left, I had no idea what would happen next. So I spent the rest of my first day humbling myself and committing to myself that I would ski like they wanted by the end of the next day so I could get on to what I came for: learning what no one else knew about long-distance ski jumping.

By the end of day two, I was more frustrated than ever. I had spent the whole day doing everything I could to learn what the kid was trying to teach me, and all I had done was frustrate him. Day three was no better, and I was beginning to think I should have left on day one. By day four, I had frustrated the kid so much that he asked another coach to try and help me. That coach quit on me after a couple of rounds and grabbed another coach. By the end of day four, I had frustrated every jump coach at the facility, and all I was trying to learn how to do was ski properly. On the last set of day four, just before I was about to try one more time, I overheard all the coaches discussing their frustrating experiences with trying to help me. Then I saw a slalom coach named Mike Munn walk over from the slalom lake. He had overheard the jump coaches discussing me and my lack of ability to do what I was told. Mike was an excellent slalom skier and coach from England and a friend of mine, but as far as I knew, Mike had never jumped before. If he had, I had never seen it. But I heard Mike ask the jump coaches, "Mind if I take a shot to help Kenny, mates?"

They immediately responded, "Go for it, Mike!" That just about took the last bit of hope out of me. I wanted to be angry, but I was too discouraged to do anything but agree. I just wanted to get this over with and go home, and I was sure no one wanted me to go home more than the jump coaches.

Mike walked over and said, "Kenny, I want you to forget about everything every coach has told you all week long. What we can't seem to get you to do is get your body in the proper position to generate more angle to the jump and arrive at the jump in a safe, stable, and balanced position. Instead of trying to do everything you have been told, I just want you to think about one thing: I want you to pull with your left shoulder and push with your right ski when cutting into the ramp position."

I immediately thought to myself, *I can do that. That makes so much sense.* All week I had tried to find a way to get into a position, and nothing I had done had helped, but if I could do what Mike said to do, the result would be the proper position. On my first cut across behind the boat, I could feel that everything was different, and I heard the Englishman scream, "That's it, mate, that's it!" At the end of day four, only seconds after wanting to go home more than ever, I was so excited I could have popped!

Jay hopped into the boat and gave me the green light, saying, "Kenny, that is something you can build on. Tomorrow, we will work on some single-cut jumps and see how you do."

Jay wasn't happy with my jumping position, but thank God, we made much faster progress on the adjustments for the ramp work. When I left for home, Jay told me, "Kenny, if you go home and go back to what you were doing, you can expect what you have always been getting. But if you can have the discipline to go home and spend the rest of your summer working on what we taught you, then maybe you can be great one day."

I had gone to the city of Zachary to train with the US team's coach hoping to come home jumping farther than I had ever jumped in my life. My friends and boat driver expected the same thing, but instead I came home jumping shorter distances than I had since I was a fourteen-year-old boy. I came home practicing what I had learned fifteen years before—practicing how to ski instead of practicing how to eke out a few more feet on each long jump. I trusted Jay, and I knew when he told me what he did that he meant it. It was all making sense to me, so I spent the whole summer practicing skiing as much as or more than I practiced jumping. When I jumped, I jumped like I had when I was a kid. I was striving to master what I had skipped over years before. As days and weeks and months of implementing these fundamentals went by, I began seeing all the problems I'd faced before disappear. I stayed the course through the month leading up to the US Nationals tournament, even though I knew I wasn't even jumping far enough to compete. With about three weeks left before the Nationals, I started putting it all together: the speed I had learned to generate in the proper body position along with the ramp work I had spent countless hours mastering at low speeds. As I began to put these skills together, the distance of my jumps rapidly increased.

While I was learning to humble myself as an athlete and master the fundamentals of my sport, I was also fighting the fear of failing again. How well I could ski didn't matter much if I was too afraid to do it when it mattered most. Ski jumping is dangerous by nature. It was pretty wild to sit on a dock with a bunch of daredevils and see the same fear in every one of my competitors' eyes that I saw in myself, but by the time every competition rolled around, we had all dealt with and accepted that fear. That sure didn't mean we wanted to ride off in a van with flashing lights, but we sure would rather ride off in that van than walk away knowing we hadn't given our all for fear of injury. I think I rode off in that van more than anyone, and always at the worst possible times. I had accumulated months in the hospital from many surgeries and spent months in recovery, yet I never allowed the fear of another injury to cripple me. What crippled me was the fear of never achieving my dream. But the thing was, that fear of failing ensured that I would do just that when my turn came in the competitions each year.

I tried to pump myself up. I tried to convince myself I was good enough. I tried listening to loud music in my headset. I tried loving myself. I tried believing in myself, and all I got was more afraid. Even after I had humbled myself and spent time learning the basics, now that I was finally physically capable of achieving my dream, I was more afraid than ever. As I waited my turn to ski in that national championship, I watched dozens of my competitors jump and felt no one had gone far enough, until the guy before me hit the ramp. The crowd went wild, screaming and yelling. Then the distance was announced: my competition had jumped farther than I had ever jumped in my life. The pressure was more than I could bear. I remember that feeling like it was yesterday, and I will never forget the one short prayer that ripped fear out of my heart by the roots. I was so overwhelmed with fear that I gave up the fight and said these words to myself and God: *Lord, never mind the gold medal. I just want to do the best I can for you.* I thought of Christ on the cross and knew I would do more for Him than I would for my dream and that if I finished for Him, I could not fail. Win or not, it was a higher calling with no chance of failing.

My turn came in those next few minutes, and I jumped farther than I had ever jumped in my life on two out of three jumps. I was in the worst circumstances I had ever faced, and I had just been more afraid than ever.

But my dream came true. I won the national water ski tournament, and afterward, I couldn't forget that this had happened because of the revolutionary fundamental truths Jay had taught me, the scripture my girlfriend had written on my equipment, and my decision to give up on my dream and give all I had for God and Tammie, whom I later married.

Before my week in Zachary, I had always wanted the best equipment and newest tools in my game. I had wanted to be able to talk with the vocabulary of a great jumper. I had wanted to look great whether I was great or not. But then my dream of winning the US Nationals came true after a mostly frustrating week in Zachary and the humbling summer that followed. Looking back at what made all the difference was life-changing in ways I knew I still didn't fully understand.

I had mastered the basics of my sport and overcome my fear not by fighting it, like I had for years, but by giving up the fight. After that, I noticed that I preferred conversations about things that mattered and could really make a difference. I had seen that all the equipment, all the sports vocabulary, all the hype had been related to my fear; it had served as a distraction from the truth. My pride and posturing could have cost me my dream forever.

After winning the water skiing national tournament, I quit trying to climb to the top and started digging down deeper to the fundamentals to make sure I knew what they were and how they worked. I wanted to understand life's basics before I spent my life chasing goals that would be impossible for me to achieve unless I mastered the simple things first. I never had to learn any secrets after I mastered the fundamentals. They were what made everything else fall into place.

Winning the Nationals was huge for me, but being able to be my best in the worst circumstances of my career and having the heart of a champion instead of a heart filled with fear was the most life-changing thing of all. It blew my mind that after years of fighting to overcome my fear, doing everything I could to defeat it, giving up led to my freedom from fear—not giving up fighting but giving up fighting fear. Getting in the right fight. For years, I skied for my championship while I was terrified. The moment I surrendered my dream of that gold medal and decided in my heart that all I had was for Christ, fear left, and my dream came true. Chewing on this really made me dig deep into what happened. My love for Christ and for Tammie had allowed me to put aside my fear and selfishness and apply my talents for the good of others. Could it be that chasing what we desire most ensures we will never find it, but putting God and others first leads to what we desire most chasing us down? Was love something I didn't understand at all?

Love was one of those things I just kind of let loose. I figured it would grow or die beyond my control, but it didn't seem to work that way. Before, my approach had been to dress like the best. When it came to love, I had tried to appear to be loving and see what happened.

After I realized the role love had in helping me achieve my lifelong dream, I began an earnest effort to master the fundamentals of love. Instead of trying to appear more loving, like I had tried to appear to be a better skier, I decided to dig deeper and figure out what love really was. I asked myself the question I felt a great coach would ask me: What is love?

Before we can master anything, we must first understand what it is, how it works, and what, if any, control we have in making sure we do our part right. I had always seen love as beyond my control, but now I was starting to see that perhaps it was actually within my control. Feeling love was not within my control. Being loved was not within my control, but loving was totally within my control. I was also realizing that love didn't rule my life when I felt it or when someone else loved me. Love ruled my life when I loved.

After asking what love was, I wondered, "What is love's greatest enemy? What makes it hardest for me to love?" The answer was fear. Fear that my dreams would not come true, fear that I would lose, fear that I would get hurt, fear that I would look foolish, fear that I would be taken advantage of, fear that I wouldn't be respected, or fear that my love for others would not be returned. As I thought about it, I began to realize that all the fears that kept me from loving others were rooted in a focus on myself. I was my own worst enemy in my fight to live a loving life.

For months I tried to understand love, and with time I began to realize that love was not what I thought it was. It was far less complicated than I ever imagined. It was what every fiber of my being wanted to be, and it was the one thing that if neglected, undermined everything else. When I got it right, it made everything else fall into place. I began to realize that love was the basic fundamental to a strong life.

Like I had skipped over the fundamentals for years in my water skiing career, I had skipped over learning about love. I also began to observe that I wasn't alone in my lack of understanding; I knew a great many other people who didn't seem to get what love really was either. So, I set out on the journey to figure it out, never dreaming that after more than fifteen years, I would just be beginning to realize how important love is, how much sense love makes, and how love really works.

CHAPTER THREE

The Fruit and Roots of Love

Before Tammie and I got married, we attended marriage counseling with a couple from our church. One of the first things the couple told us was that it was important to know that love was not a feeling; it was a choice. When they said that, my first thought was, *Wow, that sounds pretty smart.*

But as I started to chew on it, sitting on the love seat next to Tammie, I began to believe that it sounded smart but was actually insane. I had no control over whether or not I loved the girl sitting next to me. I just did! The feelings I had for her that I did not have for others were totally beyond my control. I did not create them. I did not choose them. I did not sit around and convince myself to love her, and I certainly did not choose to love her enough to want to spend the rest of my life with her. I didn't speak any of this out loud at the time. I just thought it all through and decided that the counselors had lots of good stuff to say, but, as always, I couldn't believe everything I heard. So I disregarded their idea that "love was a choice." It made no sense at all.

Later, I came to understand that when I made that choice, sitting in that counselor's room, I abandoned the fundamentals of love much like I had abandoned the fundamentals of skiing early on. I came to a hard spot, thought I was the smartest guy in the room, and just skipped

19

over what didn't make sense. I moved on, never knowing I was skipping over the one thing that would doom everything else I did if I didn't understand it. I was right; I don't control whether or not I feel love for Tammie. I was also right that I didn't talk myself into feeling it and didn't choose to feel it. I was wrong, though, to think that the feeling of love I had for Tammie was just by chance. It wasn't at all. It was the result of the choices we both were making—mostly the ones Tammie was making. What I missed by not digging a little deeper was that the feelings of love I had for Tammie, though to some extent beyond my control, were not there for no reason at all. The feelings were not love, but they were the fruit of love.

If we believe the feeling of love is love itself, then we will fight for the feeling instead of fighting for love. We are supposed to fight for love, and we all know it, but if we think that love is a feeling, then we will fight for the feeling we want—fight to win, fight to be respected, fight to not get hurt—and destroy love itself in the process. What we are doing is fighting for what is beyond our control and, in the process, destroying what is within our control: the source of the feeling. This is a confusing topic by nature because we are all so conditioned to believe that love is a feeling; it's almost impossible to see it as anything else.

Several years ago, as I was just beginning to understand all of this myself, I wanted to help my daughter Faith's youth group understand what I had learned. In order to illustrate this concept to the kids, I decided to use a tree. In my illustration, the roots of the tree represented love, the tree itself represented the miracle of how God works, and the fruit of the tree illustrated the feeling of love. I explained to them that a tree with healthy roots produces healthy fruit, and a tree with unhealthy roots produces little to no fruit at all. We talked about how no one knows or fully understands how a tree turns dirt and water into fruit. That was and is just the miracle of how God works. A healthy fruit tree planted in good soil somehow takes the nutrients from the ground and makes fruit. If you want to take that tree's fruit, simply pulling it all off the tree is not the answer. Though it may look bare for a season, if the roots remain healthy, then next spring all the fruit you took and more will return. The only way to stop a healthy fruit tree from remaining fruitful is to cut off its healthy roots. Some trees you can even cut to the ground, but if the roots remain strong, in time the tree will regrow and produce fruit again. If you kill the roots, not only will the fruit die but it will not return the next spring or ever again.

I showed this group of eight-year-old children a tree with the roots representing the seven things love is according to 1 Corinthians 13 and asked if this tree would be fruitful or fruitless. They all said fruitful. After that, I showed them a tree with dead roots representing the eight things love is not, according to the same passage, and asked if this tree would be fruitful or fruitless. They all responded that it would be fruitless.

As the children related to my illustration, I realized that we might actually be on to something. Over the next few months, as I used the illustration with the kids, I began to learn about love and see it in ways I had never considered. So many things began to make sense, and in the many years since then, my life and my understanding of it have changed completely. Where so many things never made sense, now they added up perfectly. Here again is the tree I used to illustrate what love is, what fear is, how they work, and how to make sure love, not fear, rules our lives. This illustration has helped me so much and still helps me today. I pray it will help you master the fundamentals of the most powerful force on earth: love. In this life, the right fight is the fight to have love rule our lives, not the fight for the feeling of love. Fighting for the feeling of love destroys the roots of the tree that creates the fruit or feeling of love.

This illustration labels the roots and fruit of two trees. In the Bible, 1 Corinthians 13 tells us that the seven attributes of love are: patience, kindness, truth, protecting others, trust, hope, and perseverance. It also lists eight things love is not: envy, boastfulness, pride, rudeness, self-seeking, anger, unforgiving, and delighting in evil. So a person who lives the seven things that define love would be a loving and fruitful person. A person who lives out the eight things that love is not would be a selfish, fearful, and fruitless person.

Just for clarity, I don't believe that feeling angry defines a person as angry, that feeling envy defines a person as envious, that feeling unforgiving defines a person as unforgiving, and so on. It's when we act on these feelings that they begin to define us. I have never met a person who is completely fruitful, and I have never met a person who is completely fruitless. Most of us are somewhere in between—hopefully more fruitful than fruitless. What is most important is that we are in the right fight: the fight to have love rule our lives, not the fight for the feeling of love. I think it's undeniable that a person who fights to live the seven things that define love, whether they are loved by others or not, will be a mostly fruitful person. I also believe that a person who fights to be loved by others will become the eight things that love is not and will end up, for the most part, a fruitless person. Although fighting the right fight is a good thing, fighting harder when in the wrong fight only leads to more destruction. When we fight for the feeling of love—something beyond our control—we will inevitably end up letting fear rule our lives and becoming the eight things that define fear, not love.

The fruitful tree in the illustration represents a person. For the purposes of the illustration, imagine that the person has total control of their roots and no control over their fruit, except to the extent to which they can influence their fruit by having healthy roots. In other words, healthy roots result in healthy fruit.

In this picture, the tree is completely fruitful for two reasons. First, the roots or foundations of love provide nourishment to the tree. They can do this because they are connected to and drawing nutrients from good soil, which provides water and food for the tree to grow. If patience, kindness, truthfulness, protectiveness, trust, hope, and perseverance are the roots of love, they are rooted *in* Christ. When a person is rooted in Christ and growing in Him, their roots remain healthy, feed their tree, and produce the fruit of blessings in their lives. A healthy relationship with God is the soil that grows everyone's tree of love. By choosing to allow God to nourish the seven things love is in your life, people give themselves the best chance to be fruitful and guarantee that love rules their lives, whether or not they have fruit.

Circumstances in a person's life or another person *can* take away a person's fruit temporarily. This is the second reason the tree in the picture is completely fruitful: because this has not occurred. Unlike nurturing their healthy roots, a person cannot control whether or not someone takes their fruit. These next illustrations show what can happen when a person is hurt, either by circumstances in their lives or by others.

In the case of this next tree, most of the roots are still drawing nutrients from a relationship with the soil (Christ) and thus remain connected to love. This person remains as loving as they have always been, but someone else has made a decision to hurt them and has taken a significant part of their fruit. This tree did not deserve it, but someone else—who certainly didn't have all of his or her good roots connected— has taken from them, hurt them, or offended them in some way.

When speaking to children or young adults about all this, I show them a completely fruitful tree and tell them, "This is you." Then I delete a portion of the leaves and fruit from the tree and say, "Someone took this from you."

Most commonly, the students respond that they would try to get their fruit back. I ask them if they would be patient in striving to get their fruit back, and most people say they probably wouldn't be. At that point, I show them how that decision will cut off the root that produced the fruit to begin with. I tell them that the fruit would have eventually restored itself, if one of the tree's roots had not been cut off from love.

The questions and answers continue: Would you be kind as you tried to recover what was taken from you? The most common answer is no, they wouldn't be kind. So, I show them that if they are rude, they will also cut off another root that was giving them the fruit to begin with and that would have restored the fruit had they kept it connected to love.

Then I ask, "Would you be truthful when you tried to recover what was taken from you and be willing to seek real truth?" They answer, "Probably not," because they feel they don't have to be truthful to someone who hurt them. So, I show them that if they are not truthful, they will also cut off another root that gave them the fruit to begin with and that would have restored the fruit had they kept it connected to love.

Then I ask them if they would protect others when they tried to get back what was taken from them, and again, they say they probably wouldn't. So, I show them that their choice will also cut off another root that gave them the fruit to begin with and that would have restored the fruit had they kept it connected to love.

Will they trust when they go to get back what was taken from them? The most common answer is, "Not likely." So, I show them they will then cut off another root that gave them the fruit to begin with and that would have restored the fruit had they kept it connected to love. By now, they are beginning to see and understand how this pattern is unfolding. Nevertheless, I press on.

The next question I ask them is if they will demonstrate hope when they go to get back what was taken from them. Normally, they say they actually wouldn't have a sense of hope and optimism in such a circumstance. So, once more, I show them that lack of hope will also cut off another root that gave them the fruit to begin with and that would have restored the fruit had they kept it connected to love. They replace the root of hope with a fearful boastfulness and a false projection of strength. They begin to harbor unforgiveness.

Then I ask them if they would persevere in love when they tried to get back what was taken from them, and most tell me they would have very little love left in such a situation. So, I show them that lack of perseverance would also cut off another root that gave them the fruit to begin with and that would have restored the fruit had they kept it connected.

Talking to children about this subject has taught me as much as anything. I will never forget how, after I explained this illustration to my daughter's youth group, one young boy, who was about ten years old, raised his hand and asked, "Mr. Kenny, what would we do with the fruit if we got it back? Won't it already be rotten? We can't put it back on the tree, can we?"

I thought to myself, *Wow, how true is that?*

This ten-year-old boy was teaching me that not only do our efforts to get back what was taken from us cut off the source that created it in us to begin with but what was taken cannot be restored by getting it back anyway. In other words, the people who hurt us can't restore us, and we can't restore ourselves. Although being loved is nice and makes it so much easier to love, being loved does not heal us. Only persevering in love can and will restore us.

This is because when a person allows fear to rule any aspect of their lives, what they are doing is cutting off their connection to God in that area. Instead of trusting Him to provide for them and nourish them through their struggles—whether the struggle is spilled ice cream in a new truck or being unjustly fired from a needed job—they decide to take control of that aspect of their lives. Their roots stop taking nourishment from God and wither as a result. When a person stops living in God—who is love—they cannot sustain the love in their lives that produces the blessings of fruit.

When someone offends me or does anything else that hurts me, it is impossible for that person to restore what they took. It is also impossible for me to restore what they took. What is gone is gone. The fruit, even if recovered—like that ten-year-old told me—is no longer any good. It was actually intended to be consumed to begin with.

You see, fruit in our lives provides blessings, and God has not given us these blessings in our lives just to stagnate and spoil. The fruit is in our lives to fill a purpose, and that purpose is to bless our lives and the lives of others. So, what people take from us, even when they shouldn't, is never more than what would have eventually perished—and never more than what love will restore in some way if we have the courage to live love in our own lives.

Think back to the story I shared about Grace spilling the ice cream in my new truck. The truck was my fruit or blessing, but I was afraid of having it damaged. The ice cream was already spilled, and whatever damage was done couldn't be undone.

Sacrificing Grace by screaming at her and making her feel bad would not have restored my truck. Even if she had thrown the ice cream on purpose to destroy my truck and disrespect me, love would have had a responsibility to ask why and help her to change. Ice cream in my truck would be of little to no consequence compared to my daughter being so disrespectful; discipline would have been required, but for her own sake, not because she had messed up my truck. The whole purpose of the truck was to bless my life and the lives of my family members. With time, whether I use the truck or not, it will age, break down, and eventually be discarded. All that could happen more quickly if the truck were not driven, and, in that case—worst of all—the truck would have served no purpose.

Our blessings can only serve a purpose when we share them and expose them to loss. The only other option is to protect them from everyone, and that simply guarantees they serve no purpose and will be wasted.

Now, if someone steals your property, that person can return it, but the offense doesn't go away even if the property is returned to you. You are still hurt because the theft was wrong. The best we can possibly do when we get hurt—when someone or something takes our "fruit"—is to remain loving, keep our roots connected to God's love, and persevere in love ourselves so that the roots that created the fruit to begin with will have every chance to restore the fruit. The worst thing we can do is to stop trusting in God and cut off all our loving roots from Him in an attempt to recover something that can't be recovered anyway.

Fences of Fear

When I first saw the illustration of the tree, my first thought was the same thought many others often have: Can't we live loving lives while at the same time fencing off our fruit so others can't take it?

These fences, in life, are the lines we draw to protect ourselves from the selfishness of others. We draw these lines or boundaries because we don't want to pay the price love is willing to pay—but there is no way to live a loving life and protect ourselves at the same time. In the Garden of Eden, God didn't put a fence around the Tree of the Knowledge of Good and Evil. If He had done so, He would have taken away Adam and Eve's ability to choose trust and obedience—to love of their own free will. We are not kind or trusting or hopeful when we put up fences or draw boundaries to keep others out. We deny them their chance to choose love.

When I became a father, one of the first boundaries I drew was to demand that my children respect me. I had two goals: one, to be respected as a father by my children, and two, for my children to live a respectful life. However, the boundaries I drew communicated to my daughter that she had to respect me or she would be punished. She learned her father would not tolerate disrespect—and, by example, to fear and guard against others disrespecting her as well. The problem was that was not my goal. I did not want her to be afraid or defensive. My goal was for her to be respectful. By demanding respect and punishing my children when they failed to respect me, I created distance in our family and fear and anger in my children.

However, as a three-year-old, my daughter Faith was tough, and like most parents, I hated to punish her. As she continued to be disrespectful, I began to wonder if punishing her was worth the fight. That got me thinking deeper about what I was doing and why I was doing it. Eventually, I realized I couldn't care less if she disrespected me so long as I did not have to punish her. I loved her. But when I thought of her growing up to be a young lady that was disrespectful and thoughtless of others, there was nothing on earth that I would not endure to prevent that.

The light came on for me then. Punishing Faith for disrespecting me as her father was enforcing a fence I had created out of fear. Punishing

Faith so that she would not live a disrespectful life was love. From then on, I never told her she was not allowed to disrespect me. Instead, I told her I loved her too much to let her be disrespectful. Before, I had lectured Faith on all the things that were and were not respectful to me. I lectured her on how to respect me and how I would not tolerate her being disrespectful toward me. After I took down my personal fence, I told Faith I couldn't care less if she hurt me, but I could not tolerate her being disrespectful because of what it would cost her later. I shared with her examples of how disrespect leads to destruction. I made sure she knew that I didn't like to punish her but that I loved her too much to allow her to do things that would hurt her.

It may seem that there is not much of a difference. My daughter still went to time-out either way. But I say the difference is life and death. It's not what we do but why we do it that determines whether love or fear rules our lives. When we love others, we don't have to draw boundaries or put up fences. We do what is best for them first, always, without regard for ourselves. When I loved Faith, no boundary was ever needed for me to be respected. My love for her protected me as well as her in the long run. When I failed to love her, the only way I got respected was to demand that respect.

Building fences in between you and the people who may hurt you may not necessarily protect the blessings in your life, but it will certainly cut your roots off from the love that produced those blessings in the first place. Love always costs us something, but it will never cost us as much as what not loving will cost us.

When I was asked about building fences for the first time, it was by someone in my daughter's youth group. I responded, "OK, let's see what happens," and I drew a fence around the tree. I asked the group, "Are we being kind when we fence others out? Are we being patient? Are we protecting others?" Soon, we saw that the fence destroyed our own fruit instead of protecting it. We can't fence in our lives to keep others out and live a loving life at the same time. Either we have a fence and live a fear-ruled life, or we take the fence down and live a life ruled by love. Those are the only two choices we have.

The only way to restore our fruitfulness when our blessings are taken from us is to take our fences of fear down and reattach our roots in love. Winning in life or keeping our fruit from being stolen by circumstance or by others that offend us is beyond our control. Part of life's trap is striving for fruitfulness by focusing on the fruit. When we focus on the fruit (the feeling of love and winning), we neglect the roots and position ourselves to fail.

Don't misunderstand: wanting to be fruitful or wanting to win in life is perfectly normal. Striving for fruitfulness is also OK. We just can't let ourselves become so distracted by the fruit that we ignore our roots, and we need to know that any action that requires cutting off our roots in an effort to get back what was taken from us or to protect our fruit in life will, in the end, only hurt everyone around us while it destroys us.

WHO DEFENDS US?

If we don't build fences around our fruit to protect it, then how do we defend our fruit and ourselves? When and how should we act defensively and defend ourselves? I honestly think the answer is never. This does not mean we become doormats for selfish people. Allowing people to run over us is not loving. It is selfish on our part—a fear that others will reject us if we oppose them. When a seemingly loving decision leads to allowing others to take advantage of us, it is no longer a loving decision.

If someone physically harms you, they are so ruled by fear that they are dangerous, and allowing them to harm you is not loving them. It is helping them destroy themselves and hurt or destroy you. The most dangerous people on earth are those led by fear. Loving a fearful person means not allowing them to abuse at any cost, even if it means physically stopping them—or leaving, never to return again. The person being abused does not control the abuse or cause it and must immediately exit the relationship for everyone's sake.

We will discuss how to be loving in abusive situations more in chapter 14. In most cases, if someone is physically hurting us, love demands that we protect ourselves and them by removing ourselves from the situation. Abuse harms everyone involved, and love does not allow others the opportunity to destroy themselves.

But if no physical harm is in the picture, then I don't think there is ever really a good time to defend yourself. So, the question then becomes, who will defend you? The answer is that love and the truth will defend you. Love forces us to address abuse, but it does matter how we address the abuse. Fear will stop people from running over us to save itself. In fear, we do what is best for ourselves without regard for others. Love will stop people from running over us so the other person won't destroy their own life by their abusive actions. Fear's way of stopping people from running over us destroys us in the process and hurts the person running over us. Love's way of stopping people from running over us strengthens our own roots and gives the other person the best chance to change.

The last person on this earth you want to spend your life defending is yourself. It's a twenty-four-seven job that won't end until the day you die and that leads to your own destruction. Defend the truth (one of the seven things love is), and you will find yourself defended. If that means I am the one who needs to change, then the best thing for me is to change. If the truth means someone else needs to change, then I have a responsibility to do all I can to help them change. In the end, if they won't change, I may be forced to walk away, but in all circumstances, the truth defends me, and I no longer have to defend myself. That revelation in my life was perhaps one of the most freeing revelations I have ever had.

Love grows from truth. One of the seven roots of love is truth. If someone is truly offending us, I believe it's for one of two reasons. Either this person is not living a loving life, or we are not living a loving life. If we are the ones not living the way we should, then we must change to reconnect our own roots. It's the only option, or we can count on being fruitless.

On the other hand, if the other person is not living a loving life, then we have a responsibility to defend the truth for his or her sake, not our own. The worst thing we can do is to silently watch or to enable someone to cut off his or her own roots and call that loving them. If we do that, we are not loving them, but we are helping to ensure their fruitlessness. Being truthful takes courage. Many times, subtle hints are enough to communicate the truth, but in the end, no matter what it takes, truth must be communicated.

We defend the truth in love for someone else's sake, not our own, and we are defended in the process. If I am going to defend the truth for the sake of someone else, and that person is the one who needs to change, I also have a responsibility to defend that truth in a way this individual is most likely to hear and understand.

If a person begins to sense that you are defending a truth for his or her sake, he or she will be more likely to listen and may even change. On the other hand, if someone senses you are defending the truth to defend yourself against him or her, he or she will (unless courageous) likely reject you and your words and never deal with the truth. People sometimes reject the messenger, so they never get the message. If they are afraid, they may even reject the message and the messenger, no matter what you do. The best you can ever do is to speak the truth in love, doing all you can to share the truth for the other person's sake—not your own sake—and in a way that gives them the best chance to receive it.

If people are ruled by fear, they will reject the messenger to avoid the truth; but if people are courageous, they will hear the message regardless of the messenger. Someone courageous will take the truth in any form from any messenger at any time. The problem is that we are all afraid. Some more and some less, but fear is a part of all of our lives. What determines the course of our lives, though, is not the fear we feel but the fear we act on.

We Are Not Locked in Our Fearful Choices

Every time we make a choice to act, either in fear or in love, our actions define us at that moment. If we choose to act in anger, then our anger defines us in that moment. If we feel angry but do not act on that anger, then our anger does not have to define us at that moment. If we choose to act in love and show kindness, no matter how we feel, we are defined as kind in that moment.

Our choices and actions result in consequences that often outwardly define us and pose limits to our lives, but the choices and actions we have made and will make don't indelibly lock in our identities. When our hearts change and our actions change, what defines us in that moment changes, for better or worse.

We each find our purest identity and our value in Jesus. I think Jesus defines us as all equal, all worthy of His dying on a cross. Not one of us is so much as a tiny bit more or less valuable than another. He loves us all unconditionally. He hates our sin, but He loves us; and, more than anything else, all of us want to be loved.

If we get this fundamental belief wrong and live with a misdirected sense of identity, we are broken at our cores. Only the truth can ever fix us—nothing more, nothing less. If we believe we are even slightly less valuable than anyone else, we are broken. We excuse ourselves from acting on love and loving, because we think our love and our actions don't matter to anyone; but that mentality leads to a life of fruitlessness.

If we believe we are even slightly more valuable than anyone else, then we are also broken, while the world tells us we have self-confidence. The world tells us to love ourselves. With that mentality, we feel justified to use people to get what we want. We will play to win, be led by fear, love to be loved, and, in the end, we will only have ourselves; and we are terrified. We lead lives of false pride and lies. Our fake selves require tireless self-affirmation, and our perpetual self-centeredness leads us to destruction and fruitlessness.

If we believe Jesus that none of us are deserving but that He made us worthy of His love through His own death, we are simply grateful. We know we have nothing to do with our worth, because our value is in Him. We know the truth: we are undeserving, but we are loved anyway. We know and understand we are not so much as a tiny bit more or less valuable than anyone else. We value others' needs above our own. We love out of the well of love in us, through Jesus, for the sake of others, without regard for ourselves—just as He loves us. In the end, we find that well never runs dry, only grows and flows into an endless ocean.

OUR FEAR CAN BECOME A SELFISH SHIELD

When we are afraid, many of us use our fear as a selfish shield we hide behind to protect ourselves. We defend ourselves instead of letting faith in Jesus and loving truth defend us. Fear is a selfish emotion, and when we act on fear, we act in selfish ways. I am not talking about a mean-spirited selfishness, but a fearful selfishness. I am afraid, so all I see is myself and my fear. I no longer consider others. It's all about me. Because fear tempts us to go this direction, it takes courage and faith to say that even though I am afraid, even though I am hurt, even though none of this is fair, even though I did nothing to deserve the loss I have suffered, even though people may think things I wish they wouldn't—I am going to set myself aside and consider the truth and others before I act.

You see, the only person I can ever lovingly sacrifice in any situation is myself. That takes courage because sacrifice will always cost me something, and normally it costs me right now.

Likewise, what it costs me may be gone forever, but if I pay the price, my own roots will remain connected. Whatever it costs me will return, if in no other way than in the form of new fruit in my life—because my good roots remain connected. You see, in life, if you reap the benefits now but it costs you later, then almost without fail you have made a fearful decision. But if your decision costs you now but you reap the benefits later, you most likely have made a loving decision.

Fearful decisions are deceitful. A friend of mine often says it like this: "Fear will take you farther than you wanted to go, it will keep you longer than you wanted to stay, and it will cost you more than you wanted to pay."

Forgiving Others in Love

Another fearful choice that we can often make is trying to retrieve our lost or rotten fruit instead of making the sacrifice love requires. But if you think about it, until a sacrifice is required, we don't even know if we have strong roots or not. Almost everyone will return love for love, and even strangers are normally kind at first. It is when things get more difficult and things go wrong that a person's true love or lack of love is proven.

When we are offended, a sacrifice is required. It's not an option. We have to either sacrifice ourselves and persevere in love anyway or sacrifice the person who has offended us and take his or her fruit. The problem is that it's impossible to take from others without cutting off your own roots.

This is the concept of forgiveness: sacrificing yourself in order to keep loving others when they have offended you. Jesus said that all of the law is summed up in two commandments: loving God and loving your neighbor. In essence, the law *is* love, meaning that everyone should act in a loving way toward everyone else. When people hurt us, we get angry, not just because we're in pain but because we know on the inside that their behavior was wrong. When we are treated with hate or disrespect or insensitivity, it is "taking our fruit" in that an injustice has been committed against us and something that belonged to us has been stolen, whether that something is the courtesy we ought to have received from another human being because love is the law or whether it is the blessings that have been given to us.

After we have been hurt in this way, the person who has taken our fruit has become a "debtor" or a "trespasser" against us, meaning they owe us payment for that debt or trespass—a fine for what they have taken from us. This is the sacrifice that must be repaid somehow, because that is what justice demands. We can take this sacrifice from the people who have offended us—in enmity and rudeness or in some other way. However, if we do this, we break the law of love ourselves. In order to continue living under the law of love ourselves, we have to forgive the debt we're owed—absorb the "cost" of the debt ourselves by a personal sacrifice—seventy times seven (which is to say, as many times as we need to do so).

It takes courage to forgive others. When I show students this illustration, I often ask them to look at both trees and tell me which tree is afraid and which tree is courageous. They always say that the fruitful tree is courageous and the fruitless tree is afraid. I agree.

Then I ask them how to make the fruitless tree courageous. They want to add fruit, but to add fruit, we must change the roots. I used to wonder what the Bible meant when it said perfect love casts out fear. Now I completely understand. If I feel afraid, then I am tempted to protect myself. If I protect myself, I do that initially at the expense of others. Ultimately, it is at my expense because I have severed my own roots and become a fruitless tree living a life ruled by fear.

So, how do I change that? I forgive those that have offended me and persist in love at any cost. I want to be clear: there always is a cost *to* doing this, but when I continue to let God's love rule my life, the seven things that love is stay strong, the blessings of fruit return, and fear is forced out. Just as God's word says, perfect love really does cast out fear.

CHAPTER FOUR

Living Inside Out

The choice between love and fear and the consequences attached to this choice apply to every aspect of our lives, including family, parenting, business, and athletics. Nothing is exempt.

The good news is that everyone can choose love over fear. The simplest actions and daily decisions we all make show us the fundamental rule of life we choose to live by: love or fear.

These decisions ultimately rule our lives and define who we are, whether we know and believe it or not. When it comes to choices we make concerning ourselves and others, the only choice we ultimately have is to love or to fear. We can't simply love or not love. We don't have the option to not love, as if there were a neutral place where there were no love or fear. That place does not exist in any life. If we don't act on love, we will act on fear. They are our only two choices.

I have never met a mostly selfish or fearful person who is truly fruitful or a mostly loving person who is truly fruitless. You can add love to nothing, and you will have everything, or you can take love away from everything, and you will have nothing. Likewise, you can add fear to everything (personal wealth and possessions, success, etc.), and before long, nothing you have will mean anything. Few people are completely selfish or fearful, and perhaps none are completely loving. The more fearful and selfish a person is, the more fruitless his or her life is destined to be, and the more loving a person is, the more fruitful his or her life is destined to be. The problem is that love and fear are perhaps the most misunderstood principles, even though they are so vitally important to our lives and ultimately determine who we are and what our destinies will be.

My dictionary defines love as "a profoundly tender, passionate affection for another person; a feeling of warm personal attachment or deep affection, as for a parent, child, or friend; sexual passion or desire; a person toward whom love is felt; beloved person; sweetheart."

I think those definitions describe how most of us interpret love, but I don't think they show us the whole truth. I think the truth is that these definitions capture only the feeling—what you might call the fruit of love—but not love itself.

It helped me so much to see what love really is, how it works, where it comes from, and how to make sure it ruled my life. I think it is vital that we all understand love and live it, because the opposite of love is fear, which leads to selfishness, and the last thing any of us really wants is for fear to rule our lives.

Love doesn't just respond to what people do. Love seeks to understand the thought behind the action. That is where the truth is hidden. We must ask ourselves why people do what they do before we respond. It's not what we do but why we do it that determines if something is loving or fearful and selfish. This means that in order to live a loving life, we must see life inside out instead of outside in. Love always seeks the truth, and the truth is almost always hidden.

By seeing life inside out instead of outside in, I mean that we should, first, consider the reason why someone is doing what they do. The best way I know how to explain this is to ask that you consider how you see yourself. Most of the time, we know why we do what we do, and many times, if we are not careful, we expect people to respond to why we do what we do instead of what we actually do. If we see life from the outside in, we only see what people do without considering why they do what they do. If we live outside in, we care most about what people do and how their actions affect us, without regard for why they act in a certain way. The problem with that is that even the best response is not effective if it's a response to something that isn't even true.

In other words, when I respond to someone's actions without considering why they are acting the way that they are, I may have a false understanding that can't help resolve anything or bring true understanding that helps me make a wise decision. But if I take a moment to love others as I would want to be loved, and if I choose to live life inside out, I will ask myself why I think someone may have done what they did before I respond. If I am really courageous, I will ask the other person about it. Then I can respond to the truth instead of just how someone made me feel.

Let me give an example of a time I made the mistake of living outside in. One time, I was very frustrated with a waitress that seemed absentminded as she waited on us. I misunderstood her as someone who didn't really care. It was my birthday, and my family and I were at my favorite restaurant. I only get to go once a year because no one else in the family likes it. I eat salty, fried crabs and normally drink several large drinks, but this time I found myself sucking on my ice most of the time. Tammie and I also noticed that two young girls that seemed to be under ten years old were sitting by themselves, unattended, at another table nearby the whole time we were eating. Many times, I almost got up and complained about not having my drink refilled. I wanted to yell across the restaurant at our waitress for more tea, but, thank God, I did my best to control my own anger. Since my family and I always share Shield of Strength necklaces inscribed with scripture with many we encounter, I normally leave one for our waiter or waitress when we dine out. That day, I hadn't planned to leave one behind, but my kids insisted I leave the waitress a heart necklace with this scripture on the back: "Create in me a pure heart, O God, and renew a steadfast spirit within me," from Psalm 51:10.

After we left the restaurant, the owner chased us down in the parking lot and told us the waitress was crying in the back and couldn't pull herself together to thank us. The owner then said, "Your waitress lost her husband in a car wreck two weeks ago. Today was her first day back at work, and the two girls sitting next to you were her children."

I was humbled and amazed. My selfishness had only thought to respond to the waitress from the outside in without considering what she was dealing with on the inside. Thank God my children saw her from the inside out.

46

I could give hundreds of examples of how much trying to live inside out has helped me make good decisions and build relationships instead of making foolish decisions and destroying relationships. Maybe the most important thing I have learned is that most of the time, when someone acts rude, they are simply afraid. If I react to the rudeness, I end up in a fight over a lie. If I ask why, for their sake, or just love them anyway, I normally find I totally understand the reason they were rude. Many times, I find that if I were them, I wouldn't have been as kind as they were.

It's important to keep in mind that if you stop and consider the truth first, the truth can change your actions. When I explain all this, I try to show that whoever took from you or hurt you for what seems like no reason did not define anyone but themselves by their actions. You, as the injured party, have had something taken from you, but if you stay rooted in love, that cost will be restored.

Sometimes, the kids I talk to about all this ask, "Can I be rude, mean, or unforgiving to the person who offended me but not to everyone else?"

If the person who has offended you, for whatever reason, is defined by their actions, you are equally defined by yours. It is impossible to be rude, mean, or unforgiving to the people who offend you but not to everyone else unless you can be two people. If you are angry at someone and act upon that anger, in that moment, you are an angry person. If I feel rude toward anyone and act on that feeling, then I am rude. If I feel prideful and act on that feeling, then, at that moment, I am prideful. I am letting my fear-based feelings control my responses to others, and so fear rules my life until I choose to say I will be loving at all costs.

The question the students really want to know the answer to is whether they can be unloving (and let fear rule their actions) only when they are offended and not be defined by these unloving acts. The answer to that is no, because eventually everyone will offend us, and it's only when we are offended that we show who we really are inside. No one knows what is inside of them or what is inside of others until they are called upon to give of themselves or sacrifice.

CHAPTER FIVE

Choosing Fear

Fear is defined in the dictionary as "a distressing emotion aroused by impending danger, evil, or pain, whether the threat is real or imagined; the feeling or condition of being afraid." Like the definition of love, I believe these words define the feeling of fear but not the action or the decision.

Fear is a little different from love in that love is an action or a choice that results in a feeling, whereas fear is a feeling that can result in an action. I think the trap we so often fall into is that we live based on feelings, and since feelings are often the result of other people's actions or our experiences, those feelings are really beyond our control until we realize what really is in our control.

If we don't know what love really is and how it works, we may think we are acting in love when we are really acting in fear. The eight things love is not are also the eight things fear is. If we are acting on fear, we are no longer loving. So let's now take a look at the eight things that define fear as illustrated by the tree below:

1. LOVE IS NOT ANGER (FEAR IS)

Anger is something we all feel, and those angry feelings are often beyond our control. I have never figured out how to stop feeling anger. Acting on our angry feelings, though, is something we often can control. We can feel anger but still choose to be kind. Fear acts on the anger that it feels. Anger does not rule our lives when we feel it. Anger only rules our lives when we choose to act on it.

For example, not long before I made the first Shield of Strength, Tammie and I were in the car, headed to her parents' house. Tammie was talking on the phone, and I was trying to tell her to tell the person on the phone something I needed them to know. I kept saying what I needed, but Tammie was trying to listen to the person on the phone. After a few times, I felt like Tammie was just ignoring me, so I reached over and tapped on her to get her attention. When I did, she tried to push my hand away and accidently stuck her finger in my eye. When she did that, for some reason, I lost it on the inside. I wanted to rip the steering wheel off the dashboard and shove it through the windshield. It was not rational, and I knew it, but my feeling of anger was overwhelming. I didn't do that, of course, and thank God I didn't. Had I made that negative choice, the anger I felt would have defined me in that moment and would have continued to do so until I repented and sincerely got in a fight to change. That evening, I spent a lot of time chewing on what the heck was wrong with me and decided to do my best to fight my angry feelings instead of trying to justify them. We are always either fighting our selfishness—and fighting for love—or justifying our selfishness and feelings and allowing fear to rule our lives.

2. Love Is Not Rude (Fear Is)

As in the case of anger, just feeling like we want to be rude does not make us rude. But acting on the rudeness we feel, doing what we want without regard for others, and speaking our minds without regard for what our words will communicate to others make us rude. We can feel rude yet still choose to act in love without regard for ourselves. I could go on forever about the times I wanted to be rude and was so glad I wasn't because nothing was as it appeared. I can also tell many stories of allowing fear to rule my life, of being rude, and of regretting it so much.

During Hurricane Harvey, while rescuing all the people we could, my family came to a roadblock where an officer ran us down. He was flashing his lights and using his sirens. We had been driving around roadblocks for days and had been allowed to without resistance. When this officer forced us to stop, I knew he was going to tell us we could not go in. I was ready to tell him that we had been running rescue for days and were going no matter what. I was prepared to tell him to write me a ticket and mail it to me or come arrest me, but we were going through anyway. I almost opened my big mouth and was rude based on all my assumptions before he said, "Sir, I have an address with elderly and children that no one has been able to get to yet. Will you please go here first?" As he gave me the address, all I could think was thank God I hadn't opened my foolish mouth! Since I waited to act upon my rude feelings, the police officer revealed the truth of why he had chosen to stop us. Love always seeks the truth, but if we are too quick to act on the rudeness we feel, it will define us.

3. LOVE IS NOT ENVIOUS (FEAR IS)

Feeling envy is a temptation. Just like anger and rudeness, feeling envy does not give envy permission to rule our lives. It's when we choose to continue to think on the envy we feel, to speak the envy we feel, and to act on the envy we feel that we choose to let that envy—instead of love—rule our lives.

Envious feelings pop up all the time in all people. The difference between envious people and loving people is not whether they feel envy. They all feel it. The difference is that a loving person will refuse to act on the feeling of envy. They will refuse to play with the feelings and will just be done with them. They may still feel them, but they trust the truth, not their feelings. Envious people justify their feelings and act on them, which results in envy defining who they are.

4. LOVE IS NOT PRIDEFUL (FEAR IS)

Pride is fear pretending to be strong. Pride always projects strength because it is afraid. True strength projects humility because it is secure. Fear will push or pull others down in order to pull or lift itself up. Love will push others up even if it means pushing itself down. The key to getting pride out of our lives is being grateful.

Who are the courageous among us? Are the courageous those sacrificing others to lift themselves up or those sacrificing themselves to lift others up? Who would you choose to follow?

Feeling prideful does not mean we need to act prideful. It means we have forgotten the truth, and we must repent before we ensure our own fall. One of the most important truths I teach my own children is that they are not one bit more or less valuable than anyone else. To think we are more or less valuable leads to hurting others and destroying ourselves. Put yourself first, and you will find yourself last. Be grateful in humility, and put yourself last, and you will find yourself first.

5. Love Is Not Unforgiving (Fear Is)

Unforgiveness stops our lives on a dime. Because time keeps moving forward, unforgiveness leads to us living our lives walking backward as we keep staring at what's happened. It prevents us from focusing on what is happening in our lives. Forgiving ourselves or others is not about pretending our action or another's action is OK or no longer regrettable. There are things I did thirty years ago that I despise more today than when I first did them.

Forgiveness is about not wasting the greatest sacrifice the world has ever known: Jesus Christ, who died on a cross so we could be forgiven. Forgiveness is about saying, "I want you to change, and from this point forward, I will no longer choose to surrender my thoughts to what has happened and live my life looking backwards. I will look forward, grateful that none of us are locked in or forever defined by our pasts."

Refusing to accept God's forgiveness or to forgive others always results in hurting the people around us and leads to our own destruction.

Being loved always makes it easier to love, but we must love (forgive) whether we are loved or not.

6. Love Is Not Boastful (Fear Is)

Boastfulness is fear projecting strength. Fear always projects strength, but true strength always projects humility. The truly strong never have to make sure everyone else knows they are strong. It's not hard to find ourselves tempted to want to talk about ourselves in an attempt to make others think more highly of us. The problem is that doing this does the opposite, and we know it. The only reason we even want to boast about our strength is because we see ourselves as weak, or we fear that others see us as weak. The answer is not boastfulness or convincing ourselves we are worth as much as or more than anyone else. The answer is simply believing the truth that no one is more or less valuable than anyone else.

If someone is boastful, they are always afraid that they are somehow not as valuable as others, or they believe others think they are more valuable than them.

A note on boastfulness: We can also sometimes get gratefulness confused with boastfulness. We can, with the best of intentions, share our success or excitement with someone else, never intending to stir envy within them, but find quickly that we come across as boastful instead of grateful. Love requires us to consider whether telling others of our blessing and gratefulness comes across as boastfulness. Will it force them to fight off envy in their own life? For example, if someone wins the lottery and then goes to their friend in need of money and tells them how grateful they are, they may tempt them with envy. If the friend is really loving, they will be as excited for the winner as anyone, but that does not mean they will not feel envy. It just means they have learned not to act on the envy they feel. It means that their life is not about themselves, but is way bigger than that: it's about God and others. They will rejoice with the lottery winner in spite of their own feelings; but it might not have been kind for the lottery winner to put a friend in a situation where they would be tempted with envy in the first place.

7. Love Is Not Selfish (Fear Is)

Selfishness is the trap fear wants to lead us all into. Selfishness is doing something to get what we want without regard for others. Fear will love in order to be loved, or it will give to get. Love will love whether loved or not and give whether it gets anything or not.

Most selfishness is not intentional. It's the result of being totally distracted by our own feelings. The problem is that whether selfishness is done to hurt others or to protect itself, it is still selfishness. It still hurts everyone around it in the process of destroying itself. An act of selfishness won't destroy us, but a life of it sure will. We are always becoming either more or less selfish, depending on how much we choose to love.

8. Love Does Not Delight in Evil (Fear Does)

Delighting in evil is a major red flag, and it is a sign that fear is beginning to fully mature in someone's heart. If we find ourselves delighting in evil, it may be the last chance we have to turn our ship around. Delighting in evil allows fear to take root in the deepest parts of our hearts. Finding comfort and gaining pleasure from seeing someone else suffer is the opposite of love. Delighting in evil may also be planning and intentionally doing something to hurt someone else so that we can feel better.

Evil will intentionally harm others for its own pleasure and enjoy watching them be harmed. Evil is fear, fully matured, in which love is nowhere to be found. No one ever sets out to be evil. They just keep making one selfish decision after another until they have cut off all the loving roots in their life. They don't see their fruitlessness as the result of their decisions to live a fearful and selfish life. They see their fruitlessness as the result of people hurting them. They believe all their selfishness has been justified because they were hurt. So, in their own mind, they want to die because they have been killed by people. In some cases, they will kill indiscriminately before taking their own lives, all because they have been totally deceived. Fear rules their life. It has fully destroyed them. They imagine it is not their fault, so they delight in evil unto death. In other cases, they live to see others suffer. They manipulate and deliberately use others to make themselves feel better, no matter what it costs other people, even their own children.

CHAPTER SIX

What Is Love?

A life ruled by fear is a terrible thing. The good news is that instead of choosing to let fear rule our lives, we can choose to remain rooted in Christ and let the seven things love is lead us to respond in love no matter what goes on around us. If we respond in love no matter what, we are living life inside out, but in order to really respond in love, we must understand what love is.

As we have already said, love is a decision and an action, not an emotion. The actions of love most certainly do bring emotions and feelings, but the feelings and emotions are not the love. They are the fruit of love.

Remember the dictionary definition of love? "A profoundly tender, passionate affection for another person; a feeling of warm personal attachment or deep affection." I think a better definition of love than the one the dictionary offers is this: "Love is an undefeatable benevolence, an unconquerable goodwill that always seeks the highest good of the other person, no matter what that person does." Love is self-giving and gives freely, unselfishly, and unconditionally without asking anything in return, and it does not put a limit or a trade-in value on the giving.

All this is a choice, not a chance. True love is not ruled by emotion. If people treat you in the loving way I have described, then you will feel what the dictionary defines as love. That feeling is not love. It is actually a blessing—the fruit of the love in their lives that they share with you freely. If someone loves you in action, you will feel love for them.

Just as an example, if you asked me if I love my wife, Tammie, I would tell you that I love her with all my heart. If I am talking about the feeling of love as the dictionary describes it, then what I am really saying is that Tammie loves me—she acts in loving ways toward me that make me feel warm affection toward her. But if you want to know whether I *truly* love Tammie—whether I am loving in my actions toward her or not—you need to ask her.

I feel warm affection toward Tammie—the popular definition of love—because she is patient, kind, truthful, protective, trusting, hopeful, and persevering toward me, more often than not. If she began acting angry, rude, envious, prideful, selfish, unforgiving, and boastful and started to delight in evil, you could check with me in a year and see how much tenderness I still felt for her.

My feelings of love for Tammie might be gone in such a situation, but if I truly love her, how she treats me won't affect how I treat her. I may not feel loved anymore if she stopped loving me, but her decision to stop loving me would define her, not me. But if I stopped loving her after I felt hurt, if I stopped choosing the seven things love is, then the decision to stop loving would define me as well.

The whole world can love us, but if we don't love, then love won't rule our lives.

If you know anyone who is the seven things love is, then you know they are fruitful; and if you know anyone who is the eight things love is not, you know they are fruitless. It's undeniable. We can have nothing the world has to offer and still live a fruitful life. We can have all the world has to offer and still live a fruitless life. The following seven descriptions help us to understand the roots that grow love and what love really is.

1. LOVE IS PATIENT

It is easy to be patient when we feel patient, but what do we do when we don't feel patient? When we are stuck in a line or trying to explain something to someone who just is not getting it? If we let love rule our lives, we don't have to feel patient in order to be patient.

What is patience? Patience is having the courage to take a deep breath and look for the truth even when we don't feel like it. It is being willing to wait even when we want to move on or hurry up and get what we want. Love ruling your life will require you to be patient. Above all, what we can't do is simply accept that we are not patient people.

I made that mistake so many times. My own father tried and tried to teach me patience, but I was certain I could not be patient. I said I was simply "not a patient person." I just wanted to get it done. I wanted results, and I wanted them now. I didn't care how anything worked; I just wanted to know how to use it to get what I wanted. My lack of patience as a ski jumper landed me in hospital after hospital. It slowly undermined all my efforts and all but ended my dream of winning a national championship many times. Eventually, after enough suffering and enough hurt, I had to learn to be patient whether I felt patient or not. I finally learned that if I took the time to act out of love, the fruit produced by patience would take care of itself in time. Patience is a long, steady push in the same direction, whether it seems like something is working or not. It is trusting the truth no matter how you feel. It doesn't mean we ignore the truth and keep pushing no matter what; that is foolishness. It just means that when we know the right thing, we stick with it, whether it works today or not, next week or not, next month or not, next year or not. We stay the course at all costs, knowing love never fails. Our patience should come from our belief in the truth, in love, and in God's Word.

2. LOVE IS KIND

I have rarely met anyone who isn't kind to those who are kind to them. Only those whose lives are totally ruled by fear might choose to be unkind to those who are kind to them. But if we want love ruling our lives, we must be kind no matter how others treat us.

Being kind when we don't feel like it can mean a couple different things. Sometimes it just means what it sounds like: being kind and doing the right thing, putting others first even when they are not kind to us or when we don't want to. There is another type of kindness, though, that is so important. This is the kindness that means being kind even when it does not mean being nice or polite. Letting others have their way all the time—indulgence—is often mistaken for kindness and love. In reality, it is selfishness and fear. Kind is always nice—in the long run—but niceness in the short run may not always be kind. If we are not careful, our *feelings* of love for someone will keep us from really loving them. For example, nothing makes me happier than seeing my children happy. If I am not careful, I will let them get away with living a selfish life because stopping them would require dispensing with short-term niceness and indulgence of everything they wish to do. This may hurt their feelings, which in turn hurts me. Allowing them to be selfish to spare myself the pain of hurting their feelings is not love; it is fear and selfishness.

Sometimes, kindness means allowing others to experience pain that will make them stronger and help them live a more loving life. Sometimes, kindness means holding others accountable even when it may hurt their feelings. Allowing those in our charge to give in to their selfishness or disrespect others because we claim we are protecting them is not kind at all; it is putting them on the path of living a disrespectful life.

Being kind is doing what we believe is truly best for others, even if it hurts right now or costs us something.

3. LOVE IS TRUTHFUL

Being truthful means more than just telling the truth as we see it. It means having the courage to look for the real truth. Love doesn't just respond to what people do. Love seeks to understand the thought behind the action because that's where the truth is hidden. Fear will speak its mind without regard for the truth, or how the words wound, or how they might be received and without asking the question of why someone does what they do. But the why often reveals the truth.

Love always seeks the truth. When we know the truth, we can speak the truth in love—not angrily or hurtfully but in a manner that will most likely be meaningfully received by the one who needs to hear it. And many times, in searching for the real truth, we find we are the ones that need to change.

My first thought every time I get hurt is that the person who hurt me doesn't care about me or, worse, wanted to hurt me. Most of the time, neither of these is true. Most of the time, when we get hurt, people had no intention to hurt us and hoped we would not get hurt. Most of the time, they are fighting their own fears and distracted from the truth of the consequences of their actions. Sometimes they have considered them and truly don't care or are rejoicing in evil and did want to hurt us. The most powerful part about asking why someone did what they did before we respond is that it helps us find the truth, whatever it is.

But when we ask others about their motivations, we must be sure we seek the truth in love. If we ask for answers out of anger, pride, or any of the things fear is, most people will simply respond to protect themselves and the truth they don't want to share. If we ask for their sake, we may just learn the real truth.

If, through seeking, we learn that a person who has offended us intended to do so or does not care that they did, we can thank God we know that, because if they won't change, we may need to run while the getting is still good. If the real truth is that they actually do delight in evil, we surely need to hit the road and maybe try and love from a distance. However, if, as is most likely, the hurt and offense were unintentional, treating the person as if they were intentional won't solve any problems or help us or the other person. The most dangerous people in the world are people ruled by fear. When fear fully rules a life, it's a very dangerous thing. In most cases, though, the truth is not what we first think. When I know someone is doing what they are doing not just to hurt me but because they are afraid, it really makes it easier for me to love.

4. LOVE PROTECTS OTHERS

Protecting is doing what is truly best for others. So often we think we are loving others by protecting them from truths that would help them become a better person because we don't want to see them hurt. This is the reason people tell "white lies" or withhold the constructive truth. But because we know love is always truthful, we can also know that this is never really the loving thing to do, and such "protection" is not consistent with what real love is.

Protecting means doing what gives the person we love the best chance to grow closer to God and to leave behind their own fearful and selfish ways. A protecting love tells others what they need to hear, not what they want to hear. Protecting love also protects others from physical harm. If anyone has ever protected you, then I am sure you felt loved by their protective actions, especially if that protection required they risk their own well-being.

When protecting others with our words, however, it is so important to make sure what we tell others will protect them and not just hurt them. The truths we tell should serve to build up and strengthen the people in our lives—otherwise, they do not protect them. I have told people things that hurt them when there was really never any reason for them to know. I have seen people share things with others that only caused them worry and suffering.

Protecting people means doing what is truly best for them, not just doing what would make us feel good. The one thing we can protect others from more than anything else is our own fearful and hateful words and actions. Envy and pride will tempt us to protect ourselves or even hurt others for our own sake. That is not what love does.

5. Love Trusts

The first thing we want to stop doing when we get hurt or someone takes our fruit is stop trusting—both God and the person who has hurt us. We want to put up fences and draw boundaries to protect ourselves, but we can't put up fences and draw boundaries and love at the same time. If we love, we trust; and if we don't trust, we don't love. When we put up fences and boundaries, we are seizing control of our own lives for fear of being hurt again instead of abiding in God, but it is His grace and provision that keeps love strong in our lives and that gave us its blessings to begin with. God's grace is sufficient for us. We must believe in His restoration in order to continue to live in love.

Doing this does not mean allowing someone to constantly take advantage of you. If someone is abusive or hurts you again and again, they are hurting you and destroying themselves. Love them enough to tell them the truth about what they are doing, and if they won't stop, love them enough to walk away so they do not continue to hurt themselves with their unloving acts.

If you stay rooted in God and His love, you and your fruit will be protected much better than cutting off love in your life can ever protect you. But you can't act out of love for yourself, or it ceases to be love and becomes selfishness instead. You must be loving for the sake of others.

When I was twenty years old and working my way through college, I worked for my cousin Mike Vaughan. He gave me a gravy job, paid me well, and taught me the ropes of business. We had been friends and hunting buddies for years, and he and my family were not only good friends; we were family.

My job was delivering nuts and bolts for Mike's business. Part of this meant that I refueled the truck I drove each day. At this time, I was pinching pennies and doing fine but wishing I had more money for more gas so I could run around more on the weekends, so I got the great idea of bringing a five-gallon can with me to fill when I filled up the company truck. I planned to drop off the five-gallon can in the bed of my truck so I would have extra fuel for the weekend.

I knew that this was wrong, but I didn't think it would hurt anyone, and I never once considered I was stealing from Mike. As crazy as that sounds, that's just how fear works: it justifies what it wants. In my mind, it wasn't "Mike" that I was taking the gas money from; it was the company, and five gallons of gas meant nothing to the company, right? But five gallons led to more, and one day, when I was filling up, another driver pulled up on me. He didn't say anything to me, but he asked Mike if he knew I was filling up that gas can. When I heard, my first thought was that the other driver was a jerk for telling on me. Mike fired me for stealing, and I left angry, but I knew it was my own fault. I was terribly ashamed and expected Mike, his wife, Debbie, and their two children would never forgive me. Months later, I received my typical Christmas card from their family, and Mike invited me to go hunting. I was so excited he didn't hate me but still never expected Mike to forgive me or ever trust me again.

That was some thirty years ago now, and though I took a long time to accept forgiveness, neither Mike nor Debbie ever once treated me differently. Mike loaned me his boat after that day I shattered his trust in me. He and Debbie just kept loving me like family, and they chose to keep trusting me. I always felt so ashamed each time I saw Mike, but he always acted exactly like nothing had ever happened. He loved me anyway. Mike and Debbie forgave me and showed me how to love after being hurt. They showed me trust is a choice. They can't have felt trust for me after I stole from them and broke their trust, but they chose to extend trust anyway.

It takes courage to keep loving, but when you know God is your provider and you love at all costs, you will always be better protected by loving than you could ever protect yourself. All these years later, Mike and I are the best of friends. We still hunt and fish together. Every time I see Mike, I am reminded of his willingness to love and trust me after my mistake—and also to hold me accountable through firing me in the first place. Mike's love for me makes me say I love Mike because he loves me.

Trust is a choice. I can choose to trust someone whom I have no feeling of trust for whatsoever. Choosing to trust anyone always means we take a risk of being hurt again. The feeling of trust will come and go with the actions of the people around us, but the choice to trust is ours, and we must choose to trust. If someone constantly takes advantage of our trust, the problem is not our trust but their actions. But the answer is not to have less trust, though it may not be wise to trust them anymore. If a person is continually unloving toward us and continues to abuse our trust, we are not helping them by allowing them to continue to hurt us and destroy themselves. When they will not change, the solution is to lovingly walk away—still encouraging them to change—so they can no longer hurt themselves with unloving actions. Live in hope that they will change, but for their sake, stay gone until they do. As we do this, we must continue to trust everyone else in our lives. We must not become people who no longer trust others because of a bad experience with one person or organization. We should always use wisdom in how we trust, but if we decide we will no longer trust, then love will no longer rule our lives.

6. LOVE HOPES

Hope is choosing to believe the truth that no matter what, if we persevere in love, then God will go with us and see us through. Hope is believing that with God all things are possible. We must keep the fires of hope alive in our lives!

Keeping hope alive is not about convincing ourselves we will win or survive. Hope is not believing in ourselves or convincing ourselves we can get what we want. If our hope is in ourselves, we are destined to lose it.

One thing that has helped me most with keeping hope alive in my own life is coming to realize that I have no idea what God may do next. Knowing I could be one step, one moment, one break, or one decision from everything changing helps me keep hope alive. Hope is never dead just because we lose it sometimes. Hope is never further away than the tips of our fingers. It is lost only when we refuse to love again no matter what.

I almost lost hope once. I had spent fifteen years chasing a dream. I had given everything I had and found it wasn't enough. I knew I wasn't enough, even though I tried to trust and act on God's Word no matter what. I had lost my hope many times and seen Tammie help me restore it. I had quit and tried again and quit again and tried again until it was embarrassing. I had tricked myself into believing I was the best and no one could beat me, only to perform terribly when it mattered most and be totally overcome with fear when I pretended to be fearless. I had been through it all dozens of times, and I had trained with insane, unbalanced intensity and consistency. I had done any and everything I could possibly do, including training with the world's best coaches, yet fewer than five minutes before my dream was going to come true, I lost my hope.

I had taken literally thousands of jumps as a skier. I had spent months in the hospital and endured multiple surgeries, all for my dream of winning a national championship, but one jump before my dream would come true, I lost my hope. I lost my hope because, for a moment, I put my trust in myself, and I was insufficient. I looked at my circumstances and saw I had damaged equipment. I knew I had only one jump left. I knew I would have to jump farther than I ever had in my life. I knew I had just crashed and lost all my concentration attempting to repair my equipment in the two minutes allowed; I was not able to do so. The one thing I knew everything about was ski jumping, and I knew it was not possible to do what I needed to do to win in the circumstances, so I made the only rational decision I could: I chose to be thankful for second place.

Then I saw the scripture Tammie had written on my ski handle: "I can do all things through Christ who strengthens me." I remembered I had told God that whether I won or not, I would do the best I could for Him. After a fifteen-year journey, I decided fewer than sixty seconds before it was too late that I would finish for God and trust the scripture Tammie had reminded me of so many times and had written on my equipment. My hope was not that I could win but that I could finish strong with and for God. Sixty seconds later, as I was falling from the sky at a distance from the ramp I had never sailed before, I was overwhelmed with excitement and joy and disbelief. I could not believe what had really just happened. I could not believe that I had been so wrong. I was so grateful for having finished strong even when I knew it wasn't possible. That day taught me that to have hope in myself or lose hope through trust in myself is the most foolish thing I can do. We never know when God is about to move, when love is about to break through, when everything is about to change if we keep hope alive. Hope is an anchor for our souls!

7. LOVE PERSEVERES

I have heard it said that winners never quit and quitters never win, but so many winners have quit so many times along the way. The greatest memories in any victory are the times we got back up after quitting. In my fifteen-year journey chasing my dream, the moment it came true may have been the best moment in the journey, but it was only a moment. The journey was where all the value was, and the most valuable moments were the ones in which God and others helped me get back up and try again. The only chance we ever have to persevere is when we find ourselves wanting to quit or after we have quit.

As I waited my turn to jump hundreds of times over many years, I began to learn I had little to no control over how I felt as I waited, and I also began to learn that how I felt had little to nothing to do with how I would perform. Sometimes I would feel like my body was itching to go. I felt like I could jump over the moon. Other times, it felt like my legs were made of cement, like I hardly had the strength and energy to even put my gear on. Many times, I allowed how I felt to impact how I performed when it shouldn't have. My legs feeling like concrete didn't make them weaker, and my legs itching to go didn't make them stronger. It was the preparation, not how I felt, that determined if my legs were strong or not. The problem was that how I felt still affected my mind-set.

One day while waiting my turn, feeling like my legs were concrete, I realized the only chance I ever had to practice overcoming that feeling was when I felt it. I couldn't practice persevering through that feeling when I felt great and didn't want to quit. I could only practice overcoming when the opportunity presented itself. Before long, I longed to feel those concrete legs again so I could prove I could overcome them, and what I learned in the end was that how I felt was so unrelated to my ability to perform. I started almost longing for the concrete legs because I wasn't sure I didn't perform better when I felt them.

Persevering means keeping on—perhaps quitting but always starting again. Sometimes the loss is so great or the pressures are so strong that we must quit to ensure we are able to persevere. Then we must begin again—start over when we are rested and continue on with a new mind-set and a renewed heart. Persevering means falling down, failing, but having the courage, every time, to get back up as fast as possible and get back in the fight. For ourselves—in fear—we will give all we have, knowing it's not enough but still trying desperately to convince ourselves of the lie that we are enough or better than someone else. For love—for God and others—we are able to give more than we ever knew we had.

Perseverance is important in many aspects of life, but one thing we must persevere in more than any other is love. The only way love won't work is if we don't love. Love really does never fail if we persevere in love. I used to think love does fail because I saw it failing all around me. I saw marriages failing, relationships of all kinds failing, even my own relationships failing—so how could it be that love never fails? What I learned was that love really does never fail—we just fail to love. When we fail to love, then fear wins, and failure becomes our destiny.

Loving people will get us hurt, that's for sure, but it will never hurt us more than choosing not to love. Persevere in love at all costs!

CHAPTER SEVEN

Feelings Don't Produce Roots

In our lives, we experience feelings, and we take actions. Feelings come and go, most often beyond our control. However, decisions and actions are fully in our control. Our decisions and our actions can be based on our feelings, but they don't have to be. In other words, I can spend my life just reacting to all my feelings, or I can choose to set my feelings aside long enough to consider what the truth says about the situation. If we set aside our feelings long enough to respond to the truth in love, we will keep healthy, loving roots. If we immediately react to feelings in fear, we will risk destroying the love in our lives and living with the consequences.

Feelings are real, but they are often very misleading. If we make our decisions and take actions based on how we feel or how people make us feel, then feelings and other people, which are beyond our control, will rule our lives. By attempting to control our lives based on our feelings, we hand over that control to everyone and everything else that may influence those feelings—often in ways that are not founded in the truth.

Once, when I was coaching my daughter's softball team, two of the players were arguing with each other. I wanted to try and help resolve the situation, so I asked them to come talk to me about what was going on. The argument was heated enough that I decided to separate them and talk to them individually before I talked to them together. When I asked them each what they were so upset about, they both explained how the other one was being rude and insensitive. When they told me in detail the things that had happened, it was pretty easy to see why they both had had their feelings hurt. I asked them each what they'd done when the other one hurt their feelings, and they both said they'd protected themselves or they'd defended their feelings by hitting back or reacting. I asked why they'd done that. They responded that they wouldn't allow people to be rude or take advantage of them without trying to stop this. I asked them both, "Do you realize if you treat people based on how they treat you in an effort to keep control of your life, you will actually give control of your life to everyone else?" They asked me what I meant by that, and I said, "Well, if you treat people who are nice to you nicely and people who are rude to you rudely, what would you do if everyone was rude to you?" They guessed that they would be rude to everyone. I said, "So really, you will be what others determine you will be, not what you determine you will be, what the truth is, or what God says about you. Do you really want to do that?" They said they didn't. I said, "I don't want you to, either, because neither one of you is rude to me. You're both awesome and loving young ladies, but in order to stay awesome, you have to commit to always strive to be that from now on, no matter how anyone treats you." I asked if they would do their best to do that, and they said they would. We all hugged and never had another problem the rest of the season. I found out later they had been best friends for years, but their friendship was coming undone. Fear destroys relationships and, in the end, destroys us. Love builds relationships and, in the end, builds us. We are all born with the special power to love. If we love for ourselves, our special power still works, but it works to destroy us. If we love others, expecting nothing in return, then love rules our lives, and the fruit of love is our destiny.

Nothing has ever deceived me more than my own feelings. I have learned that if my feelings don't align with God's word and the truth, I should do my best to completely ignore those feelings. If they are based upon a lie, then it is better not to react to them and to let the truth replace the lie and soothe any distress I may be feeling. That's very hard to do, because feelings are strong and real.

If feelings rule our lives, then fear will dominate and drive us. That happens not because of the feelings themselves but because we allow the feelings to determine the choices we make and the actions we take. The choices we make and the actions we take truly *do* end up ruling our lives. This is not to say that we are doomed to be defined by bad choices we have made in the past that we may regret now. There is always repentance and the choice to make different decisions tomorrow, though our past histories may or may not continue to have consequences. I mean that the choices we make today and those we will make tomorrow determine tomorrow's destiny.

We know that we have feelings and make decisions and choices every day, from the time we wake up until the time we go to sleep. The trap of life is allowing our feelings to determine our decisions, giving in to a life ruled by fear.

Love holds the key to freedom from this trap or prison. Love acts without regard for feelings, and, many times, even contrary to the misleading emotions we may be feeling. The good news is that when love rules our lives, feelings follow and make a turn from the negative to the positive. If we can allow love to rule in our lives, feelings take a back seat, except for the joy we find in the courage to love and the difference that makes in the lives of others and ourselves.

Let me give you an example. One evening, Tammie and I had decided to stop at Jack in the Box for a burger. Tammie sat down, and I was waiting to order. The young man in front of me was ordering and acted like he was possibly a leader of a local gang. It crossed my mind to give him the Shield of Strength off my neck, so I was trying to think of a way to start a conversation with someone not so interested in talking. He ordered a Sourdough Jack. Because I had always wondered how those sourdough buns tasted, I decided to ask him. I said, "Hey man, how is that sourdough bun?"

He glanced my way as if to say, "I know you didn't just say something to me," and then turned back around.

My *feelings* had me wanting to say, "What the heck was that, man? I am trying to help you, and you punk me." But I just sat there for a second. I had seen a lot by this time after giving away thousands of Shields of Strength and had gotten pretty bold when it came to loving, so I decided to ask him again. Again, I asked, "Hey man, how is that sourdough bun on that Sourdough Jack?" About this time, the lady taking our orders had walked back up to the counter.

In front of this lady, he responded by turning around and looking at me. "I don't know, fool!" he said.

His hostility made me feel defensive. The first thought that ran through every fiber of my being was to say, "Well, pal, let's figure out who the fool is. Freaking punk." Instead, I fought off the feelings and said nothing.

This kind of interaction is extremely tough for me because I was raised a fighter. I would sometimes rather fight than argue. My dad always tells me, "Kenny, all this love stuff is good, but never forget that nothing will humble a man quicker than a good, ol' fashioned butt whooping." I was thinking that this guy or I needed a humbling, and quick. Instead, I ordered our food and watched him sit down and eat with his buddy, who looked angrier then he did. As we ate, I told Tammie what had just happened and pointed them out to her. We all finished eating at about the same time and walked out right behind them. We got in my truck, and I noticed they had probably walked to the restaurant. There was no housing close by, so I knew they had walked a while. Then I told Tammie I was going to try one more time. I grabbed four Shields of Strength, two for each of them, and ran them down as they were leaving the parking lot. Tammie didn't want me to go, afraid that I would get hurt, but I figured I could outrun them both. I'm not the fastest guy on the planet, but I tend to think I am, and I figured that running for my life from these two guys, if I had to, would make me a little faster.

When I approached them, they seemed caught off guard. I immediately began speaking and said as humbly as I could, "Hey, can I give y'all something? These are some things I make with a few of my favorite scriptures on them. These scriptures have helped me through things I wouldn't have found my way through without them." I was looking at the chains as I put the dog tags on them, assuming they would take the necklaces but watching out of the corner of my eye for them to react in fear or more anger. They didn't say anything, but their body language said they would like to have them.

I handed them the Shields of Strength, and as I turned to walk away, one of them said in a kind voice, "Who are you?" It was as if he were really asking, "Why would you do such a thing for someone like us?" His wall of fear and projected strength had just shattered into a million pieces, and he stood before me in the truth of who he really was. I told

75

him my name and that I was someone who had spent most of his life living in fear, until God's Word helped me see the truth. I prayed it would do the same for him.

Before I left, I said, "Trust God's Word no matter what, and I pray His peace will always keep you." As I walked away, I realized that what could have been one of my worst experiences in sharing Shields of Strength had just become one I would never forget. I realized that my initial response to their anger was responding to a lie with a lie. Their lie was who they were pretending to be. If I had acted according to my feelings, I would have been reacting with a lie of who I was. The truth was that we were all vulnerable, and we were all afraid. I left more committed than ever to no longer live a fearful, fake life but instead to seek the truth at all costs for the sake of others, even if it cost me everything.

It takes great courage to act based on love when our feelings so desperately tempt us to do something different, at least at first. But if you live out courage long enough to experience the freedom and fruit of a loving life, the courage becomes natural, and you become more afraid of being selfish than of being selfless. Once love rules your life, you realize you don't want to go back to the old, fearful behavior. Once you see your willingness to love at all costs making a difference in someone else's life, loving becomes easier. Not to say it is ever easy, but who needs easy when we've got Jesus?

Take another look at the illustration of the fearful and loving trees. Study them, the fruit and the roots, and let your understanding of love and fear find a new perspective. Remember: love is an action that results in feelings, and fear is a feeling that will, if we are not careful, result in actions that are not loving and can even destroy our lives.

Whether your life is ruled by love or fear is not determined by feelings. It's not determined by your circumstances, and it's not determined by how others treat or have treated you. It's determined by actions and choices you make, no matter how you feel—solely by what (and who) you allow to rule your heart. Remember that if you keep your roots connected to the love of Christ, the fruit or blessings of your life will take care of themselves.

I'd like to distinguish between the blessings in our lives and material possessions. The fruit, or lack of it, represents how productive and full or how unproductive and empty our lives are, not how many things a person may have. A fruitful person can have few possessions or many possessions, but their life is peaceful, and their relationships are healthy. A fruitless person can have few possessions or many possessions, but even if they have an enormous house and the nicest car, their possessions bring them no joy or peace, and their relationships are sick, just like their tree.

The fruitful tree reflects a loving life in which a person has kept their roots healthy, drawing from God's love to make loving decisions. The abundant fruit on the tree reflects the feelings of love and being loved that result from living a loving life. The roots are the decisions that feed and grow the fruit, fed by the actions a person takes every day to allow God's love to rule their lives. Their fruit is the harvest of those actions.

The tree on the right shows the fruit that results from living a life driven by fear, comprised of fearful acts (those eight things love is not but fear is). By reacting out of fear instead of trusting in God's love, the roots have withered. They are broken and starved and have produced no fruit at all. If you know anyone who is mostly the eight things love is not, then you know they are fruitless, regardless of what they own or don't own.

Our roots are 100 percent within our control. People can make us feel anger, but people can't make us act on that anger. People or situations can encourage feelings of pride or envy in us, but nothing and no one can control how we act or don't act on those feelings except us.

We decide whether we keep our roots connected to God's love, whether we feed or destroy them. No one else can do this. Others can make it easier or more difficult to make the right decisions, but they can't force us to make the wrong decisions, no matter what they do or how much they have hurt us.

What others do to us is only temporary, unless we make it permanent by allowing fear and how others make us feel by their actions to cause us to cut off our roots from love. Our reactions to others' behavior can cause long-term damage if we choose to live fearfully, with our choices and actions motivated by a desire to protect ourselves from future pain because we are afraid of being hurt again. The worst thing that can happen to us is not that we get hurt, no matter how deep that hurt might be. The worst thing that can happen to us is that after being hurt, we stop loving and allow fear to begin to rule our lives.

It's also important to remember that while our roots are fully under our control, our fruit is not. In other words, people can hurt me and take my fruit if they want to. That would have nothing to do with my roots but everything to do with theirs. I control my roots but do not control my fruit, except to the extent that I can influence my fruit through my roots. Always remember that our responsibility in life is not to our fruit but to our roots and to the fruit of others—a responsibility not over whether they live a fruitful life but to increase the blessings in their lives, adding and not subtracting from their fruit by treating them with love. Our responsibility is to help them love by loving and to make sure we don't take the good fruit they produce by our selfishness.

CHAPTER EIGHT

Religion or Love?

I've mentioned God and the love of Christ many times in this book. You may be asking, "So I need religion to make sure my life goes well?" Actually, no. Once, a pastor I know and respect told me he didn't like religion. I didn't understand at the time. My first thought was that he didn't like Jesus. I couldn't believe it. But as time has gone on, I've learned he didn't mean that at all. He had tapped into a truth I hadn't grasped yet. Religion is giving to receive something. Love is giving and expecting nothing in return. Luke 23:39–43 tells us that when Jesus was hanging on the cross, there were two men hanging with him. One of the two men mocked Jesus, and the other of the two men defended Jesus. The first man said, "Are you not the Messiah? Save yourself and us."

The other, however, said in reply, "Have you no fear of God, for you are subject to the same condemnation? And indeed, we have been condemned justly for the sentence we received corresponds to our crimes, but this man has done nothing criminal." Then he said, "Jesus, remember me when you come into your Kingdom."

And Jesus replied to him, "Amen, I say to you today you will be with me in paradise."

I don't think the sinner on the cross defended Christ thinking those words would get him into heaven. He expected nothing in return for his kindness. At that moment, selfless love ruled the man's life. When Jesus responded, that man may very well have forgotten he was hanging on a cross.

Religions operate from an exchange or bargain perspective. If we follow a certain set of rules or principles, we can ensure we live a good life, improve our position in the next life, attain enlightenment, or earn a place in heaven. Religion works for a reward, but as we have established, love works for others. Focusing on the rewards of living a loving life is one of the best ways to make sure those rewards wither and die.

Some say all religions are equal, but that is only possible if all religions are false. So let all religions be equal. I propose that Christianity is not a religion. It's a relationship with the one and only God. I believe the truth proves it. True Christianity is actually the opposite of religion.

In Christianity, what we do doesn't matter as much as the reasons why we do it. The key to living a life of love instead of living a religious life is seeing life inside out by being grateful for the truth and by giving but expecting nothing in return. The Bible says we love God because He first loved us. God is love. If you find yourself doing things for God in order to receive something in return, spend time thinking about what He already gave, and if you're not sure what He gave, read about it in the Bible in the book of John. You may find yourself falling in love with a God who already loves you.

The difference between love ruling your life and religion ruling your life is the difference between life and death. The Bible says you can do everything to gain something and receive nothing, or you can love God because He loves you, expecting nothing in return, and get everything. I would hope if God never gave me a thing or saved me from any pain that I would still love Him for what He already gave.

Shadrach, Meshach, and Abednego from the Old Testament exemplified selfless love for God. These three Hebrew exiles were placed into a furnace because they would not deny God. The Bible says God delivered them, and they didn't even smell like smoke, but they were not certain going in the furnace that their faithfulness would be rewarded. Their last words before they were thrown into the furnace were, "Our God will deliver us, but even if He doesn't, we will not bow to your idol, O King."

I hope I have the faith to believe my God will deliver me and the courage to say, whether He delivers me or not, I will still love Him no matter what trials I am faced with. I also hope I will love my wife, my children, my friends, my neighbors, and even my enemies, whether they love me back or not. If I can find that courage, love will rule my life, and if I can't, fear will rule my life. These are the only two options.

True Christianity is a relationship with the one true God, the source and foundation of all love, that gives us the power to keep our roots connected even when we are alone or offended. By surrendering, humbling ourselves, accepting love—which is Jesus Christ—into our hearts, and filling our minds with His Word, our hearts are filled with the power to live out the love God gave us on the cross. This is what it means to connect your roots to the source of their life. God's love fuels love in your life, which brings about the blessings of love, joy, peace, and healthy relationships with others, not as an end goal but as a byproduct of a life ruled by love.

I don't think it's possible to love unless we know we are already loved. If we are loved but have no idea we are loved, or if we are loved and don't believe we are loved, we will live a selfish and fearful life. Modern psychology knows this, so its approach is to teach people to learn to love themselves as the source of the love that they can then share with others. It teaches that until we love ourselves, we can't love anyone else, but this is not the truth. It's right when it says we can't share love we don't have, but the problem is that self-love is no substitute for being loved. Actually, self-love is the opposite of love. It's fear-based. If love is doing what is best for others without regard for ourselves, then self-love is doing what is best for ourselves without regard for others. This decision not only doesn't help us love; it actually ensures we kill all the love in our own life. It leads to our own destruction.

The answer to believing we are not loved is not to love ourselves. If we just think about it, we all know attempting to love ourselves as a substitute for being loved is insane. The answer to feeling we are unloved is simply to accept and realize the truth of how loved we really are. To understand and accept the love of Jesus Christ, who gave Himself and His own life for us despite our sin. The answer is coming to understand that in spite of our selfishness, in spite of our fear, in spite of our manipulation, in spite of the fact our sin was the whole reason He had to go to the cross, He went anyway. He did what was best for us without regard for Himself. He loved even when He wasn't loved, He gave even when all we did and still often do is take. He died on the cross in our place when in no way, shape, or form did we deserve it.

When we really realize how we are loved despite not being lovable, despite our own selfishness, and accept the love of Christ into our hearts, then and only then do we find a never-ending well of love in our lives. When that truth drops into our hearts, we no longer want justice; we want mercy. We no longer want our way; we want love's way. We no longer want to love ourselves; we want to take up our cross and sacrifice ourselves to a life of learning to love like Jesus loves. We no longer love to be loved; we love because we are loved. Whoever tries to keep their life will lose it, and whoever gives their life away will find it.

What a relationship instead of a religion means is that if someone never had a chance to read the Bible but loved Jesus Christ with all their heart, everything else would take care of itself. On the other hand, if someone knew every word in the Bible and worked hard to live it only for their own reward without consideration for others, their life would be ruled by fear. The Word of God actually says that a person can speak with the tongues of angels, have the faith to move mountains, and give everything they have to the poor, but if they have not love, they have nothing.

All people of every color, of every nation around the world function the same way—which I see as proof that there is one God, one Creator. You can take a sampling of people from anywhere in the world who speak or don't speak, hear or don't hear, are cultured and educated or have never been exposed to civilization—of any color, any race, any demographic—and their hearts, minds, and bodies will all work fundamentally the same way. They reject selfishness and embrace love.

When the religious people were looking for Jesus to crucify Him, a man named Judas agreed to lead them to Jesus for thirty pieces of silver. Judas agreed to kiss Jesus on the cheek to reveal who Jesus was, so the religious people could take him for crucifixion.

You may have heard people say that Judas sold Christ for thirty pieces of silver. I also thought that was true for years, until my friend explained that Christ was not there to be sold. Christ was there to make a purchase. It was not possible for Judas to sell Christ. Judas only had the power to buy or sell himself, and the same is true in our lives. We cannot be bought or sold or valued by others' actions or decisions. Their actions or decisions at the moment they take the action or make the decision define them, but those actions and decisions say nothing about us. Of course, others' actions and decisions can cost us something, but it's our actions and decisions that define us to others and ultimately direct us to fruitfulness or fruitlessness. Judas sold himself for thirty pieces of silver, and he realized it only after his betrayal led to Jesus's crucifixion on the cross.

In contrast, Christ's purchase, His love for us, gives us all the hope for change. Our lives change when we love Him.

Nothing in this book will be of any value to anyone unless they first love Jesus. God is the soil that nourishes the roots of a loving, fruitful life. In fact, if a person loves God, learns His Word, and puts others first, as He commands, they will not need to know anything I have written; they will live a loving life so long as they trust Jesus and His Word.

We can do nothing apart from God. But with God, all things are possible. Coming to understand what love is and how it works served to prove to me beyond doubt that Jesus really is love and really is my Savior. I pray you will make Him yours too, because then you will have the heart to live a life ruled by love and witness the fruit of it all. We can spend our whole lives chasing what we want and never find it. Or we can put God and others first—in relationship, not as a matter of religion—and find that what we want will chase us down.

Chapter Nine

I Do, I Don't in Marriage

About a year into our marriage, I began to sense that Tammie was becoming frustrated with me. I didn't understand why, so I asked her about it. She said she didn't understand why I didn't hold her at night in bed. I told her it was because I would sweat when I held her; it was too hot.

That didn't go over well, so the next night when I got in bed, I put my arm around her. She pushed it off. I thought it was silly and that she was just trying to make trouble. I didn't say what I was thinking, but I questioned her.

But Tammie said, "I want you to hold me because you want to, not because I asked you to."

"The problem is that I don't want to because it makes me sweat," I explained.

"Then don't," she told me and rolled over to face the wall.

So, I didn't. But I felt that wall she went to sleep facing that night beginning to wedge its way between us.

A couple more days went by, and I thought more about what she'd said. In some ways, it seemed ridiculous, but in other ways, it made perfect sense. My problem wasn't that I didn't want to hold her. I didn't like holding her because I had a hard time sleeping when I was too warm. I also had to humble myself to get over being angry at the fact that it seemed she didn't care about my discomfort.

One afternoon, I prayed and thought long and hard about it all. I started the whole inside-out thinking, and I did my best to look for the truth, as love had taught me. I realized Tammie wasn't just mad to make me mad. She was hurt because I wouldn't hold her. With a little more thought, I considered that it was a blessing to have a wife who loved me enough to be hurt when I wouldn't hold her.

Then I thought about how she was the one person who had actually left her family to live her life with me and how her prayers always carried me through my trials and fears in life. She trusted me to love her as much as she loved me, and she also trusted me as her protector and partner. In this life, it was the two of us against the world, and she was my partner for life by choice. The more I thought about it, the more I realized that even though I didn't want to hold her for me, I did want to hold her for her. A little sweat or loss of sleep was a cheap price to pay for the love and life she was giving me. Heck, if I couldn't make that small sacrifice for my wife and life companion, I wasn't worth kicking.

That night, I asked her to let me hold her. After a couple of nights, we decided to lower the thermostat to sixty-eight degrees to make sleeping close together more comfortable. Except for a rough day now and then, we still hold each other most every night. To tell you the truth, my feelings get hurt sometimes if Tammie doesn't hold me.

This seems like such a trivial thing now, and I wonder why in the world I didn't just lower the thermostat in the first place. I think it's because I couldn't see the simple truth when my own fear, pride, unforgiveness, boastfulness, envy, and selfishness blocked my view.

If you don't remember anything else from this book, remember this comparison: holding Tammie because she asked me to is religion.

Holding Tammie because I want to is love. Doing things for God or others to get what we want or to follow a rule is religion. Doing things for God or others out of love that compels us to want to do those things—that's pure love.

Choosing Love in Marriage

We've discussed how love is a choice, not a feeling, but how does this work in marriage? Love and fear are perhaps more recognizable in marriage than anywhere else. When two people get married, they normally say they fell in love. If they get divorced, they normally say they fell out of love. This isn't always the case, but the vast majority of the time, it is. Of course, everyone's circumstances are different, and there can be a million things involved, but here is what I believe is fundamentally happening in a majority of cases.

Because many people are under the mistaken impression that love is a feeling, they are understandably upset when this feeling fades. They do not know how to get it back. Some choose to hang in there as long as possible, hoping the feeling will return. Others let go, convinced they cannot "fall back" in love.

But as we have seen, love is an action and a choice that results in feelings, not a feeling that exists on its own. If a married couple who has "fallen out of love" and is waiting for the love to return perseveres in making selfish, fearful choices, they as individuals and their relationship together will become more and more fruitless. In other words, as time goes by, each person in the relationship will feel less and less love as they live out less and less love, caught in a cycle that plays out the eight things love is not. They will be waiting on fruit to return, but the fruit can't return because all the roots of love have been cut off.

Here is where it gets crazy. Desperate to protect themselves from being hurt, this married couple seizes control of their roots in their fear, cutting them off from love. Each person believes it is the other's fault, for being hurtful, but in reality, each is to blame for their own long-term fruitlessness. Each partner is responsible for keeping his or her own roots connected. Neither can restore the fruit of the other, even if they want to, because they have no control over each other's roots.

We are the only ones that can decide whether our roots are connected to love or not. We can love one another and give our partners the best chance to restore their own roots, but in the end, we must restore our roots whether our partners are giving us our best chance or not. If we don't keep our own roots connected to love, then fear and fruitlessness rule our lives. If we continue to blame one another, we hurt more and despise each other more. Each day we spend waiting to fall back in love but persisting in fear, we find ourselves hating our partners more.

What is really going on? Where does the love go? Can it ever come back? If so, how do we get it back? Here is what I believe happens at the fundamental level, even though every specific case is different.

When two people fall in love, if it's really love, then it's for a very simple reason: they are choosing to be the seven things love is toward each other, even when it costs them something. Even the most attractive, charismatic person—if that person is engaging in the eight things that love is not—will not be very attractive to the other person for long.

The truth is that we don't really fall in love. We choose to love. When someone chooses to love us back, then love rules our relationship, and the fruit or feeling of love is there. Sometimes I think of it like this. If you put two people with nothing in common, with or without any physical attraction to each other, on an island, and if they are both living out the eight things that love is not, then before long, they will be on opposite sides of the island, hoping the other one is suffering—and both would be willing to die before offering the other any help. Even selfish people don't like selfish people. But if you put two people on an island with nothing in common, with or without any physical attraction to each other, and they practice the seven things love is, before long, they will be together, feel love for each other, and be willing to die before the other one suffers. They will battle to see who can love more.

In other words, loving people will feel love for a loving person. Selfish people will feel love for a loving person. Loving people may love but not feel loved by a selfish person; and a selfish person won't love or like another selfish person.

We can illustrate what happens when people fall in and out of love using the trees.

First, two people meet, and they are the seven things that love is toward each other, as shown in the illustrations. Their roots are connected to love, and their relationship is fruitful.

Inevitably, however, before long, one person will offend the other.

91

In the beginning, the person offended will sacrifice himself or herself and remain the seven things love is. Their roots are still connected to love, so what was taken from him or her will return, and the roots of both trees make it easy for both persons to love again.

But, inevitably, a second offense will come.

Again, the person offended will sacrifice himself or herself and remain the seven things love is. What was taken from him or her will return.

If the two people communicate and try to see each other inside out, they will realize that the unloving acts that caused offense were mostly fearful or thoughtless acts, not hateful ones. Their communication flushes out truth, and truth brings understanding. All of this leads to a healthier relationship where love has a chance to grow stronger.

But if communication is lacking, then truth is often unseen. In that case, before long, we tend to become weary or get tired of the same person offending us over and over again, especially when we love him or her. If we are not careful, when people offend us, instead of persevering in love, we will choose to cut off our own roots to protect ourselves. Sounds crazy, doesn't it? But that's exactly what we do.

When this occurs and one person in a relationship offends the other, then in order to protect himself or herself, the offended person chooses to be one or more of the eight things love is not.

Their partner, instead of responding in love this time, chooses to be unforgiving and rude.

Now the original offender must make a choice either to sacrifice himself or herself, apologize, and love in order to start the restoration process or, in retaliation, to protect himself or herself from the offense endured. This process can take as little as a few hours, days, or weeks, or it can take years, depending on the choices and personalities of the two people.

In the end, the results are the same.

As you can see, the fruit or love didn't just fall away on its own, even though it may have felt that way if the two people were not conscious of their actions and choices along the way. The love and fruit fell away because both people stopped choosing to love.

You may have heard that a relationship is a fifty-fifty or a give-and-take deal. I don't believe that is true. It could be if the relationship is built on dishonest manipulation, but healthy relationships built on love are built on truth.

In a healthy relationship, it is one hundred–one hundred: a give-and-give deal. Love never takes. When we understand that love is a choice, the good news is that love can come back—but not without a sacrifice of self. The only way to restore love is for both people to begin choosing the seven things that love is even though they may not gain anything at first. Love must rule each person's life before it can rule in a marriage. Each person must love even when he or she gets offended, even if that offense is because we feel unloved by our spouse.

Remember that it is never your responsibility to make sure anyone else loves you. It is your responsibility to love. We can't force anyone to return love to us. We can only give others the best possible chance to do so by loving them and expecting nothing in return. With practice and over time, people gain confidence to love without expecting a return and will find it feels safer to love, especially when they are loved back. But regardless of how it feels, we must love in order for love to rule our lives.

LOVE AND APOLOGIES

After twenty-five years together and twenty years of marriage, I love my wife more than ever, and I think she loves me more than ever as well. I don't say that lightly. I am always wondering how we could possibly love one another more, but we continue to find new ways. Practice made us better at choosing love, and we feel greater love for one another as we get better at loving. I feel love for Tammie because she loves me, and she feels love for me because I love her. As often as possible, each of us does what is best for the other without regard for ourselves, and when we mess it up, we fight to own our mistakes.

Sometimes it is not easy. But when we disagree and offend one another, accidentally or on purpose, love demands an apology to begin the restoration of the relationship. Remember: love is doing what is truly best for others without regard for yourself. That may not always be what you want, but that's what love does.

Recently, my brother Gabe approached me about buying a house to flip (fix to sell or rent for a profit). I had never done this before, and as I considered the idea, I held off mentioning it to Tammie. I wanted to wait until I was sure whether I thought it was a good idea or not.

But when Gabe emailed me more details about the home, Tammie got the message since the two of us share an email. Naturally, she asked if I was going to buy a house without mentioning it to her. It never looks good when you're caught discussing a major financial decision without yet bringing it up to your better half. I explained to Tammie that I was just considering the opportunity and that if I thought I was a good idea after learning more, we could talk about it. That didn't go over so well. Of course Tammie wanted to be a part of the process if we were buying a home, and rightfully so. I assured her that she would certainly be involved.

Fast-forward a couple of days, and I was sitting in my truck with Tammie next to me when my brother called me on speakerphone. Gabe said something about signing a contract on the house, and Tammie looked at me like, "You said we were going to talk about this."

I panicked. All I could think to do was to hang up on my brother. I couldn't explain what he was talking about to Tammie afterward, even, because Gabe had lost me the second she looked at me like I was chopped liver. Everything was a blur after that. Tammie let me have it for moving forward without her after I had promised I wouldn't. If I felt that I had done this, she would have been perfectly right, but I felt I hadn't moved forward yet, and I still didn't really plan to do so without talking more with her. But I couldn't explain this to her in the heat of the moment. After she had torn in, all I wanted to do was tear right back.

Now and again, we'll have a fight like this, in which just the right things come together to create the perfect storm, but normally, in these conditions, the two of us are not stuck in a truck driving seventy miles per hour down the highway. Normally, we can just walk away, but this time, there was nowhere to run. Around halfway into round one, I referred back to an earlier conversation I had thought we'd had, and Tammie didn't think she'd said what I remembered. When she denied the statement, I responded, "You're a liar."

Wow, was that a bad decision! Tammie is not a liar. In fact, she couldn't lie to save her own life. More to the point, words mean a lot to her, so my resorting to calling her a liar was a really dumb move on my part. I knew it, too, but in the moment, I didn't care. I was angry and let my anger carry me away.

Halfway into round number three, I came totally undone. I slammed my hand on my dashboard, screaming so loud that literally five minutes later, I had no voice left, and my hand was swollen. After my fit, Tammie screamed at me, "I don't like you!"

Even in the middle of our major fight, that made me pause. Again, Tammie is very careful with her words. I knew "I don't like you" meant

"I love you, but I don't like you right now." I suspected that what she really wanted to say was, "I hate you." I wanted to say, "I hate you, too."

Tammie wouldn't go there. Neither would I, but in that moment, neither of us liked the other. I was not loving Tammie, and she was not loving me. I was feeling no love for Tammie, and she was feeling no love for me. Roots were flying everywhere, and so was the fruit. A few minutes later, we pulled into the driveway at home.

Two days later, we still weren't speaking. But I noticed that each morning when I got up to go to work, my normal cup of coffee was still waiting for me before I left. I wondered if I should have been a little nervous to drink it.

It normally takes me longer to get over a blowup than Tammie, but I am telling you, she is the most loving person I have ever met in my life. When I saw that cup of coffee waiting in the morning, my first thought was to just leave it on the counter out of anger, but even in the middle of our fight, I knew not to give in to rudeness. Anyway, I enjoy my coffee. So I took it.

After two days of silence, I got a text from Tammie just when I was about to text her to say how much I hated not liking her. Her text didn't go into how I made her feel. Instead, it was an apology. She said how sorry she was for yelling at me and for responding without full under-standing. She did say she wanted to be included, but then she went beyond that to explain her fears: that she was afraid I didn't value her input on major decisions. I responded with how much I hated not liking her and asking if the coffee had been safe to drink. I wouldn't advise this approach if your partner doesn't know you're joking. Texting anything hateful is a major mistake, while texting loving communication in awk-ward moments can be very healing. Instead of having to suffer through another day of misunderstanding and anger, a loving text can get a lot done in a moment. A few texts later, we had both apologized for our major, stupid mistakes. When I got home that evening, she was so happy to see me, and boy, was I happy to see her too. I hugged her, not wanting to let go. I was filled with a feeling of love for her for reaching out to me and for continuing to love me despite my selfish, fearful reactions in the heat of the moment in that fight we had in the truck.

I am almost fifty now, and honestly, I am not sure I am much better at handling my feelings and emotions in the heat of the moment now than I was thirty years ago. What I have gotten much better at, though, learning from Tammie, is being quicker to repent, apologize, and stop fighting over what doesn't matter. I have learned that in any dispute, if I am only 1 percent at fault and the other person is 99 percent at fault, love requires me to address my 1 percent before I can speak to the other person's 99 percent. I have learned that, thank God, a loving life is more about the marathon than the sprint. Sometimes we fall flat on our faces; sometimes we know everyone else is flat on their face; but if we are quick to get up and love again, love will keep ruling our lives.

You know, the truth is, Tammie and I normally grow stronger in our love when we forgive one another after a major hurt. Hurt can be the bait that leads to a fearful life, or it can be the springboard to a more loving life. When Tammie and I were fighting, I felt no love for her, and I am sure she felt little for me. But when I saw that cup of coffee two days in a row and I saw her texting me she was sorry, her persistent love toward me even after my insane selfishness bore fruit: I felt a little more love for her than I had ever felt before. I think hurt followed by real selflessness is the greatest opportunity love ever has to grow.

In this life, fear wants us to put ourselves first. It does not trust God to provide and protect. But if we give in to fear, we will find ourselves last. Love wants us to put ourselves last. If we do, we will find ourselves first. What makes Tammie the most loving woman I have ever met in my life is not that she is never selfish, angry, rude, or any of the eight things love is not. What makes her the most loving woman I have ever met is that she always seeks truth, repents for her mistakes, forgives me for mine, and keeps on loving no matter what. The hurts along the way only serve to prove her love is real and will never stop. Love really does never fail. We often fail to love, but love never fails.

In life and especially in marriage, none of us is capable of living a perfectly loving life, but living a mostly loving life will depend on our willingness to apologize and repent. As we seek the truth, apologize, and change after our mistakes, we will get better and better at living a life that is more loving than fearful. We can be more selfless than selfish, and every time we blow it, we can get up to try again. When someone else blows it, our responsibility is to understand and help them see for their sake why they need to humble themselves and change.

Often, we fall into the trap of defending our own mistakes and attacking others for hurting us when they make mistakes themselves. We try to use the facts as a weapon to defend ourselves instead of using love as a bridge to find the real truth that brings us together. When we argue with our loved ones, the truth may be on our side, but our responsibility in love is to use it not to defend ourselves but to help those who have wronged us change for their own sakes. Once we deliver the truth in love, if they won't receive it, we have done all we can. We can't change anyone; we can only give them the best possible chance to change. If, on the other hand, we allow fear to rule our lives and warp the truth to defend ourselves without regard for others, in the end, we will always blow it and hurt those we feel the most love for and want to love more than anyone else. In those moments, our only hope is apology and repentance. It doesn't just save us; it builds us and others.

In marriage and in life, my prayer is that you will get in the right fights. What destroys relationships is rarely mistakes or failures to love when we are pressed into a corner or make mistakes. Any somewhat-loving person knows that everyone makes mistakes, but what most people don't do is own them, repent for them, seek the truth, and do their best to change. If we see someone willing to say, "I know I was wrong, I see how it made you feel, I value the truth more than my feelings, and I want to try again," we would be foolish not to try again, unless we have learned that they don't really mean it and are only saying what they know they need to say to get what they want. That is a terrible, manipulative situation, and in those circumstances, we may need to walk away so others do not continue hurting themselves with their selfishness and unkindness. But if we know the person who apologizes means it, we try again. We may fail again, but if the effort is real, the struggle is worthwhile. We should love the people who hurt us, own it, and desire to change all the more for their humility, and we should try to be as humble ourselves.

CHAPTER TEN

Loving as a Leader

We love not only in our families but in our businesses, as leaders in our workplaces. I've observed that before people will follow you, they will need to believe three things about you. First, they need to believe that you have some knowledge of where you are going. Second, they need to know you won't sacrifice them for the mission. Finally, they need to believe you won't sacrifice them for yourself.

Note that I am not talking about a boss. The boss is the opposite of a leader. A boss drives people, but a leader serves people. A boss pushes and intimidates from the rear, and a leader serves and encourages from the front. A boss values self and profits above all, but a leader values the truth above all. The very nature of leadership requires that people trust you enough to follow you. People serve a boss only out of fear or necessity.

A true leader understands the fundamental principles of love—that in order for any mission to be accomplished, some sacrifice is required. That sacrifice may be hard work, time, humility, or service. A true leader in a home or office, on an athletic field, or anywhere else will protect others by sacrificing themselves, and they will honor the truth.

Bossy people in a home, office, on an athletic field, or anywhere else will function with the same fundamental principles—turned outside in. They will protect themselves by sacrificing their family members, coworkers, and teammates because they are afraid. They are blind to the truth. A boss fails to realize that he or she can never boss out of others what others will freely and willingly give the organization when they know they are loved. Giving to get is not loving; it's manipulation. People can usually recognize manipulation. A boss is better off just bossing than attempting to love us to get what they want. The only thing worse than using or manipulating people is using or manipulating people with love, or, you could say, with God, because God is love.

In Business—No Competition for Love

In my hometown, there are two competing sports-and-outdoor stores. Both are large national chains. They are on the same freeway, a mile or two apart. One has the advantage of being in a complex with other major retailers. It is near the busiest intersection in town, directly across the street from the mall. That store also has a nicer facility, a more attractive storefront, a better interior, and similar pricing and products. The other store is on the outside edge of the area with the most traffic. The location is more difficult to find access to.

Even with all those advantages, 90 percent of the time, the nicer store in the better location will have one register open with no one in line, while the store with the disadvantage in location will, 90 percent of the time, have five to eight registers open with three to five people in every line.

In business school, I learned the three most important things to a successful retail business are location, location, location. But as these two stores demonstrate, although location is important, it is not the most important thing when there is competition down the street. I don't know the management of either of these stores I mentioned, but I can tell you why I believe one is struggling to survive and looks and feels like a ghost town while the other is overrun with business.

It's plain and simple—one store seems to be run with profits first, whereas the other store is run with love for the customer first. One store's operations are driven by fear, and the other store's operations are carried out with courage. The unsuccessful store stocks all kinds of gear for the outdoors for a completely different climate than our town. It stocks all kinds of fishing gear for fishing that doesn't even exist in our area. Most of that stock ends up on clearance racks. I am sure the store managers must have told corporate these items will never sell in our area, but corporate keeps sending the stock, and the store keeps filling its shelves and aisles with those items. I assume it's because upper management doesn't have the courage to listen to lower management.

The struggling store recently changed its return policy. Any item you purchase comes with a thirty-day return policy unless you pay extra for product insurance. The problem with that is that some expensive products should last far longer than thirty days, and if the merchandise fails at sixty days and you paid three hundred to four hundred dollars, the store staff will simply tell you to read their return policy. This store's return policy was created without a thought for the customers. Of course, the ideal store manager is the kind of person who doesn't like looking his neighbors in the eye and saying, "Mr. Jones, I know you bought that four-hundred-dollar item reasonably expecting it to last far longer than thirty days, but our policy says thirty days. I can't take it back."

How many times does that have to happen before the customer doesn't feel welcomed or valued? This whole culture breeds selfishness. Store managers aren't standing up for the customers but instead giving in to their own selfish fears of offending their supervisors. Everyone in management is looking out for the self instead of the customer, and that's no way to run what should be a customer-oriented business!

Not too long ago, a friend of mine purchased an item from the store with the strict return policy, and shortly after the thirty-day return limit, the item failed. He brought it back to the store, and the young lady in customer service explained it was beyond the thirty days and the store couldn't accept the return. My friend explained the item has a normal life of a couple of years and hoped for some understanding. The young lady, doing what she had been told, explained to him there was nothing she could do. He asked her to call a manager. The lady called the manager, and the manager told her in her earpiece that the item could not be returned. My friend asked the young lady to have the manager come talk to him. The manager said he was too busy in a meeting to come talk. My friend asked the young lady where the manager was in the store. The lady pointed across the store to a guy standing near a clothes rack, talking to another employee. My friend walked over to the manager and asked that the store and the manager stand behind the product. The manager said he would not.

In an organization where leadership is afraid, the organization will project strength instead of humility and stop listening to and searching for truth. It will push the responsibility of dealing with the backlash of fear and poor decisions down to the bottom of the chain of command. The CEO, a boss that rules by fear, decides to protect the store at the expense of the customer. This decision is pushed down to the regional manager, store manager, and register worker. So, the store eventually protects itself right out of business, just like a person protects himself or herself into a fruitless life.

Now let me tell you about the store with the inferior location and facility. If there is any trouble at any time with a product, they don't require a receipt. They simply happily accept the returned item, take the item to a bin in customer service, and get another one to give to the customer. I am talking about fishing rods that were clearly damaged by the customer, shoes that have obviously been worn, toys that were clearly broken by the customer, and products that did exactly what they were supposed to do—returned for exchange. All the merchandise is collected behind their counter in a packed return bin I see every time I visit the store. For some of the items returned, you know the customer should have been embarrassed to make the return.

Recently, I saw a barbecue pit that a customer returned that must have been at least two years old. The wheels were worn out. It was rusted because the paint had finally given way from the heat of so many meals being cooked on it. The sun had faded the remaining paint. I have never gotten that much mileage out of a barbecue pit. There it sat behind the counter near the return bin, proof that someone had taken advantage of the store's return policy—some selfish customer looking out for himself or herself without regard for the store. But the store management had already decided it wouldn't be defined by selfish people or acts of selfishness. Management had decided it would do the right thing, even when others didn't, and the store stood by its return policy, even in that instance. If a customer was not happy with the damaged item, they could go get another.

This store reminded me that it's impossible to live a loving life and not be taken advantage of. But this store has not given up on putting its customers first, showing leadership and love. Their policies have borne fruit in the number of customers that keep returning to the store.

On my last trip to this customer-oriented store, I asked the young lady at the register if she had ever visited their competitor. She had not.

I said, "Well, I can tell you there is one register open, and no one is in line, and there are more employees in this smaller store than there are customers and employees combined in the competitor store." Then I said, "Look at this store overflowing with people." I asked her if she knew why.

She said she didn't. I said, "It's because your store is loving and puts its customers first, and a big part of that is your return policy."

She kind of grimaced, shook her head, and said, "We take everything back here," as if to say it was ridiculous and she wished they would change it.

I said, "I know people take advantage of your policy, but your store refuses to take advantage of people, no matter who takes advantage of the store, and that's why you see all these registers with lines at them right now." I told her to always remember that example of putting others first, because it was more important than she might realize.

Here is what I suspect will happen to the better sports-and-outdoor store at some point if it doesn't remain fundamentally strong. In time, the store may be sold, or the people who built it on strong roots of love will move on or retire, and an outside CEO will take over. The first thing he will do is look at the numbers.

Now, in a business, the numbers—while important—are like fruit, not roots, an illustration of what is going on underneath. When this new CEO sees the percentage of returns at the loving sports-and-outdoor store, most probably significantly higher than in other stores they have managed, they may react in two different ways. If the CEO came from the roots or fundamentals under the numbers and worked their way up in the company, they will know immediately those returns built this business. That new CEO will defend the customers' right to returns, even at the expense of the business. But if the new CEO is afraid and wants better numbers to prove he is better than the last leadership, the CEO will change the return policy in hopes of increasing the fruit or profits. The new return policy will send more profits to the bottom line. For the first few years, it will look like a brilliant idea, so more such decisions will be made. The store managers will call and report that customers are not as happy as they used to be, but the fearful CEO will look at the numbers and respond that the company is in business to make a profit and take care of shareholders, and profits are up.

But like in other areas of life, this bossing, stemming from fear, focusing on the fruit without regard for the roots that supply it, will in the long term only rot the business from within. A good CEO, a leader, who sees that returns are seemingly too high will go to the store level and seek direction, even asking the customers what they think of the return policy. That will require more work and humility, and that self-sacrifice will require love.

Managers in businesses either boss, working from a place of fear, or lead from a place of love. Those are the only two options. I realize I am making a lot of assumptions, and I pray my favorite outdoor store continues to focus on what's best for the customer, but the opposite happens all the time in business and in our own lives. We protect the fruit at the expense of the roots that provided the fruit to begin with. When we do, we may get an immediate desired result, but the long-term consequence is the death of our roots. If your decision will gain you an immediate result with a long-term cost, it's most likely a fearful decision. If your decision will cost you immediately but provide long-term results, your decision is most likely loving. Love sees life inside out, and fear sees life outside in. Love sees business from the bottom up, and fear sees business from the top down.

CHAPTER ELEVEN

Winning and Sports

If you're not competitive or don't care for athletics, please don't skip this chapter. Sports may not be your thing, but the principles we learn in sports and competition apply to all of life, because love and fear apply to all of life.

A big reason people play sports is to achieve the dream of winning. The same is true in all of life, but like in other areas of life, in sports, if we really want to win, we need to look at everything inside out and see what will give us the best chance to truly win at what really matters most. What most people don't realize is that, largely, winning is a distraction, whether it is finally obtaining a desired promotion or scoring higher than your opponents in your game of choice. Now, any athlete who doesn't want to win may be in the wrong sport. I am not saying that winning isn't important or that we shouldn't want to win. I'm saying that if an athlete plays solely to win, he or she will be led by fear, and if a coach leads his or her team solely to win, then he or she has no choice but to lead and be led by fear—the fear of losing.

WORLD SERIES COOL DOWN

Let me give you an example of how we can see this. In 2013, the Boston Red Sox played the St. Louis Cardinals in the World Series. Both teams' batting averages were less than stellar, but the Boston team had seen their averages fall off a cliff, except for one player. That player was David Ortiz, whose stats had rocketed from a very respectable .300-plus season average to over .700 in the first three games of the World Series. Ortiz was eight-for-eleven in the series at the time and, in this game, looked as relaxed as I have seen any athlete at practice.

However, the team's average on the whole, at a time in the series when the team should have been playing their best, had plummeted to .189, which was half of their regular season average. By game five, the Red Sox had accumulated a major league all-time record of over 143 strikeouts.

It is safe to say that batters in the World Series face some of the best pitching in the major leagues, but it is also safe to say that pitchers face some of the best hitters in the league. So why in the world would the best athletes in the world be playing at only half their potential in the most important game series of their lives? As I watched, it was clear to me that it was fear. The athletes were playing to win, distracted by the pressure of their desire to achieve a lifelong dream. In our own sports endeavors and in life, if we play only to win, we will be led by fear—and the closer to our dream we get, the more undone we will become. We will abandon our fundamentals when it matters most.

In game four of the series, with the game on the line, Ortiz watched his teammates striking out, one after another. As I was watching live on TV, David Ortiz huddled his team together in the dugout, much like a football quarterback would huddle with his team on the field. The sight was something so rare in baseball, the television camera zoomed in to capture the moment. The announcer mentioned how he had never seen anything like it—a player, not a coach, huddling a baseball team in the dugout. The announcer commented that it appeared that Ortiz was trying to pump his team up.

At that moment, I looked at Tammie and said, "No, he isn't. He is trying to calm them down, baby."

Athletes rarely need to be pumped up. In the heat of competition, none of us do if we love what we are doing. We need to calm down and get back to loving, and the only way we can love our best and give our best for our sport, our team, our fans, our families, or our Savior is to focus on the fundamentals. After the huddle, Jonny Gomes went to the plate with two men on base. Jonny was then zero-for-nine in the World Series, even after batting nearly a .300 season average. Gomes hit a three-run home run that put the Red Sox over the top in game four before they went on to win the World Series.

After the game, reporters approached Ortiz and Gomes, asking what Ortiz had said in the dugout huddle. I had chills waiting to hear. Gomes told the reporter that Ortiz told them to calm down. He told them, "It's just a baseball game."

According to Gomes, Ortiz told the Red Sox not to worry about the World Series but just to play ball. Gomes said that Ortiz told them not to worry about the pitching, because the Sox were throwing strikes. Ortiz told them to go hit for each other. Gomes said the huddle helped him calm down, relax, and focus, instead of being distracted by the World Series and all that was at stake. It was most likely the exact same thing that Gomes had been taught in T-ball. But when everything was on the line—Gomes's dreams, his goals, a lifetime of training, and the desires of all his team—for a moment, he and the rest of the Red Sox allowed fear to distract them until Ortiz reminded them not to.

If we are not careful, we can also become distracted by the "m-e" in "team." Abandoning the fundamentals, giving in to fear, instead of being our best when it's needed most, we can find ourselves suddenly functioning at half our potential.

BATTER UP!

Let me share another example that helps illustrate my point. In the 2011 World Series, the Cardinals played the Texas Rangers. Lance Berkman had been a clutch hitter most of his career, going all the way back to when he was with the Houston Astros. He was a guy you knew would get a hit when it was desperately needed.

In the tenth inning of game four, the Rangers were up by one run. There were two outs, with a runner on second base. The Cardinals needed a hit to have a chance to win, and Berkman walked to the plate. If he struck out, the game was over, but if he got a hit, he would tie the game and give his team a chance to win. After a few pitches, Berkman was behind in the count and had two strikes. One pitch away from losing the game, he got a base hit up the middle to score the tying run. The Cardinals went on to win the game and the World Series.

After the game, a reporter was interviewing Berkman and asked him a question similar to this: "With a record of no World Series championships at this point in your career, this had to mean so much to you. You had two strikes, and you had to get a hit to win the game. If you had struck out, your team would have lost, yet you got the base hit. What in the world was going through your mind?"

Watching the interview, I knew that if Berkman had been thinking everything that reporter had just said, he would have struck out. I couldn't wait to hear what he was about to say. He said, "I was not thinking about any of that. I knew that the best hitters in baseball only had a one-in-three chance of getting a hit in my situation. I knew my best chance was to keep my eye on the pitcher's hand and try to pick up the pitch as early as possible. I noticed it appeared to be an inside pitch, and I knew all I could do with that pitch was try to fight it off for a base hit. I was able to do so."

What Berkman really said was that he had learned that even in the World Series, living out the pinnacle of his childhood dreams—even when his whole team needed him so badly—even when he seemed to have so much to lose if he lost and so much to gain if he won—he had learned that the best possible chance he could give himself was to set all that aside and be the best he could be for something more important.

I had seen interviews of Lance Berkman giving his Christian testimony. It was clear to me that at the critical moment in that World Series game, for his God and his team, he had put aside winning to be the best he could be at bat, allowing no other distraction to cloud his mind. What he needed was to focus on sound fundamentals. If Berkman had been distracted by the status of the World Series, two strikes, trying to be better than he had ever been in his life, or winning, he could have never picked up that pitch early enough and had the sound mind to fight it off for a base hit.

Berkman took care of the fundamentals of his sport—his roots—and the fruit took care of itself. I know that he could have done everything right and still struck out. But he gave himself the best possible chance to win by putting aside himself and his desire to win and playing—undistracted—for a higher goal: love.

WINNING IS NEVER ENOUGH

I see you sports fans shaking your heads: If you don't play to win, then why do you play? The answer is simple: although of course anyone involved in any effort wants to win, at some point, they must realize that they will give more for God, their teams, and their families than they will for a simple win.

If I give my all for God and others, then, win or lose, love rules my life. If love rules my life, then winning is really icing on the cake. If, though, I play only to win, then I will sacrifice others to win, and fear will rule my life. The crazy thing is that if I play only to win and fear rules my life, then when I do win, fear still rules my life because after I win once, then I must win again. If winning is really everything, as some say, then there is never peace, because the next competition starts when the previous one ends, and the athlete lives in a constant state of fearing failure. I believe this is why, after achieving their dream, many very successful people will say that they still have not found what they are looking for.

In leadership, if an athletics coach, boss, manager, or leader of any other sort plays solely to win, then everyone on that leader's team knows they and the other team members are expendable. In other words, winning comes before them. If a team member helps the team win, they are secure. If they don't, they are gone, so the team members play for themselves and not each other, and everyone lives in fear. Fear can motivate; but where fear motivates, it also destroys. In contrast, love motivates a team from the inside out; and where love motivates, it also builds.

If we alter the illustration we have used throughout this book to depict two teams, which team do you think is most likely to win?

The team on the left with all the fruit, of course, is most likely to win.

I am not saying a loving team that is not prepared will defeat a prepared, selfish team. I am saying that with all other things equal, the loving team wins most of the time, and many times even when the loving team is not quite as skilled as the selfish team. This becomes even truer the closer to a dream the team gets in the playoffs or major championship games, because that is when winning becomes more of a distraction and love becomes more sound minded.

At the highest tiers of sports competition, the levels of competency and physical ability of the athletes are not normally significantly different. Most athletes at the top levels of their sport are so close in athletic ability that what will almost always separate them are the factors of fear and love. Fear can cause any athlete to perform at less than his or her ability in any championship game or competition, and love can help him or her perform better.

There's More to Winning

The 2013 Super Bowl run is a great example of the concept of how love is a better motivator than fear. The Baltimore Ravens were not as physically talented as their opponents, but the Ravens' calling was higher than winning. They were playing for their God and each other, win or lose, until the last second of every game. The closer they got to the championship, the more powerful their focus on love and God became.

When the season was over, the players for the Super Bowl champion Ravens said, "This may sound crazy because football is such a rough sport, but what put us over the top was love." They told the truth! One player even said they were all ready to die for each other out there on the field.

Do you know why? Leadership emphasized teammates over winning, even though they all desperately wanted to win. The dynamic of fear is this: "If I play to win and don't win, I feel I have less value. I will play to win motivated by the fear of failing. When it starts looking like I might fail, I start coming undone."

Love says something different. If I play for others and for Christ, winning is less important and doesn't determine my worth. God made us to love, not to be selfish. Love says: "I will give my all until the last moment for my team and my Savior. If it looks like I may fail, I dig deeper, undistracted by winning."

When we play only to win, we give only as much as we perceive we have. However, for love, we can give more than we ever realized we had. If we play only to win, we begin to lack a sound mind in the midst of worrying only about losing. When we play for our teams and our Savior and think we may lose, we can maintain boldness and a sound mind. While my competitor is growing weaker (if he or she is playing only to win, which most do), I am growing stronger. None of this guarantees a win, but a love-centered perspective does give me the best possible chance of winning; and no matter whether I win or lose the competition, if I am motivated by love, I am winning at life.

I don't think God picks who wins. God always has the bigger picture in mind. I think God wants all his children to be empowered and victorious over fear so they can be all they were created to be. That's the real win in life: that we can love others so love can rule our lives and fear and sin can be conquered. It just so happens that when love rules, we have the best chance of winning, because we are the best we can be, especially against those who compete compromised by their fear.

So, next time you hear an athlete thank God, it may be that God and love did make the difference in his or her performance. I can assure you, if that player loves God, then God certainly made the biggest difference in that player's heart.

This is how David was able to defeat Goliath. David was not fighting only to win. He was fighting for his God. Goliath was not fighting for his army. He was fighting for himself. Strength always projects humility, and fear always projects strength. Goliath boasted about his might, laughed at David, and projected that his strength was so great that David didn't even have a chance. David boasted only in the might of his God. He was humble enough not to be distracted by Goliath or his own weakness. David trusted God, not himself. Goliath trusted himself, or at least, he acted that way, and so much so that he walked right into the stone from David's slingshot. Had Goliath not been so prideful, he would have been a tougher opponent. The same is true for you and me.

CHAPTER TWELVE

Loving in Your Influence

Living a loving life is important for anyone, but as a person accumulates influence, both the good and the damage they can do with their choices increases. Let me give you an example of what I mean.

A few years ago, my brother, Gabe, and our dad went to eat at a nice steak restaurant in Houston for dinner. After the two of them were seated in the restaurant, they noticed what looked like Secret Service staff guarding a back section of the restaurant. Gabe's curiosity got the best of him, and he stood up to see what he could see. Sitting in that back section were former President George H. W. Bush, his wife, Barbara, and more of their family. At that time, President George W. Bush was nearing the end of his second presidential term, so he and First Lady Laura Bush were not with the family group in the restaurant that day, but it was still very exciting for my brother.

Since our family business is making dog tags and jewelry called Shields of Strength, which have scripture inscribed on them, Gabe wanted to give one to the former president and some to his family, so he approached the Secret Service agent and asked if it was OK to approach the former president. The agent said, no, it wasn't a good idea, but if you knew my brother, you would understand that words don't usually stop Gabe if he really wants to do something. He really wanted to approach the former president. He couldn't see anything wrong with doing that because all he wanted to do was encourage the family, so Gabe decided to ask the waitstaff if the former president came in there often.

The waitress told Gabe that he did, so Gabe asked the waitress if she thought the former president would mind if Gabe approached him. The waitress said she thought it would be fine, because Mr. Bush was always really nice to everyone.

Gabe had heard what he wanted to hear, so he headed straight for the table in the back section of the restaurant, made a beeline to where the former president was sitting, and put his hand on the former president's back. Gabe never looked at the Secret Service agents when he was approaching the former president, so he wasn't sure how they were reacting, but I am sure he had their attention.

With his hand on Bush's back, Gabe said, "Sir, may I give you something?"

The former president turned around and looked up at Gabe, kindly nodded, and said, "Yes."

Gabe gave him one of the dog tag necklaces we make for the military with Joshua 1:9 inscribed on it. It reads, "I will be strong and courageous. I will not be terrified, or discouraged, for the Lord my God is with me wherever I go." Gabe thanked the former president for his service to our nation and thanked him for his son, President George W. Bush's, service to our country. The former president graciously thanked Gabe and asked if Gabe would mind repeating that message to Barbara.

Gabe walked down the table to Mrs. Bush, told her the same thing, and then gave the whole family seated at the table Shields of Strength.

I got a phone call from Gabe after he left the restaurant. He told me this story, and I began laughing at Gabe's boldness. Gabe then went on and on about how kind and nice the former president was. What impressed Gabe most was the whole family's kindness.

Here is my point to this story: when former President H. W. Bush encountered Gabe, he had great power, due to his influence, to build up or tear down my brother. If you have little or no influence in anyone's life and are rude to others, the damage is minimal. But the more influence you have, the more damage your selfishness will do. If you have little or no influence in someone's life, your kind act may have a minimal impact. If you have a great influence in their life, your kindness will have much more of an impact.

If an average person had thanked Gabe for sharing our family's Shields of Strength and been just as nice as the forty-first president was to him, Gabe would have thought of him or her as a nice person, but he would not have been as greatly impressed as he was with the former president's kindness. On the other hand, an average guy's rudeness would mean less than a president's or former president's rudeness. If the former president had treated Gabe poorly, the rudeness would have stung Gabe like a hornet. Rude or kind reception, either way, Gabe was never going to forget his encounter with the former president. I think if the president had been even a little rude to Gabe, it would have seemed to him that George H. W. Bush was the rudest person he had ever met.

You may not be the president, but there are certainly people in your life over whom you have an enormous amount of influence. Your close friends, subordinates at work, and family members may all be looking at you in different ways to see how you are living your life. Usually, our greatest opportunities for influence are with the people closest to us. But many times, if we are not careful, we will treat a stranger better than those closest to us. That's always a sad story.

Loving people, loving parents, loving friends, and loving businesses feel right to us, whereas selfish ones don't. We don't know why, but the second we walk into a loving home, a loving business, or a loving environment of any kind, we want to stay as long as we can and come back as soon as we can. On the other hand, when we walk into a selfish home, a selfish business, or a selfish environment of any kind, we want to leave as fast as we can and never come back.

Love and fear are spiritual matters, and God placed a sensor in every one of us that tells us to flee from selfishness and run toward love. I don't know about you, but I have walked into homes where I immediately felt so relaxed that I could have easily lain down on the couch and gone to sleep. But I have walked into other homes where I felt like I couldn't get out quick enough. Selfish people can act lovingly, but they can't keep you from sensing their selfishness. If someone is selfish, it doesn't matter how he or she treats you. At some point, it will cost you more than you expected.

Always remember: a selfish person will act lovingly toward you to get what he or she wants. In other words, they will love to be loved. That is not love; it's manipulation. But you will know something is wrong. Dig deeper, and move slowly into that relationship. A loving person will never have a problem with you taking your time to trust him or her. He or she will encourage you to take your time. If a person is loving toward you but selfish toward others, he or she is a selfish person who wants something from you. As soon as he or she obtains it, that person will begin to be selfish toward you.

Have you ever known a nice person who was nice until you upset him or her? He or she becomes a completely different person. You really don't know who someone really is until you offend him or her and see that person's true colors. Now, everyone will be selfish every now and then, but a loving person will repent of their acts of selfishness. A loving person will be the seven things love is the majority of the time. A selfish person will persist in the eight things love is not, no matter how much it hurts the people around them.

Our love or our selfishness has its greatest impact upon our children. There is no one we have more influence over than our own children. From birth, they hang on every word we say. I don't think we normally think about this. We are busy and have so much on our minds that we do what feels right at any one time without realizing how deep our kindness or rudeness can touch our children.

One time, I had decided to replace our air conditioning return vent. It was almost twenty years old and had slowly begun to rust. I decided, after a long day, that since it had six screws and should be simple to switch out, I had time to switch it out and still get everything else done I needed to before sitting down for the evening to work on this book. I figured the vent work would take about fifteen minutes. After pulling the first screw, I heard the door to the garage open and slam shut and then two little bare feet slapping the tile as they ran across the kitchen floor. I looked up and saw my son, Kennedy, running over with the handful of tools that Nana and Grandpa had bought him after Grandpa built Kennedy his own workbench for the garage. At the time, Kennedy was four years old and loved working on things and helping Daddy, but I knew the air vent screws could get stripped out if they weren't removed carefully, and I only had about fifteen minutes. If I let Kennedy do the job, as I could tell he wanted to do, the repair would take the better part of an hour or more.

So, I started by saying, "What are you doing, buddy?"

He looked so excited and said, "I am going to switch out the vent, Daddy. I brought my tools."

I know that, as you read this, the right decision here will seem obvious to you. But that afternoon, that right choice didn't seem so clear to me. I must confess, I was thinking, *What if I offered Kennedy a bowl of ice cream? Maybe I could just ask him to go get me another tool and pull all but one screw while he was gone . . .*

But he just looked so excited, and his excitement was making this a tough decision for me. I knew that I didn't want to spend an hour on this job, but I remembered what my friend, Tom Massey, had told me a few years before. Tom and I had just been chatting about our kids one day when he'd said, "I will give you one piece of advice, and that is, no matter how much longer a job takes, always let your kids help if they want to. They learn that way, they grow closer to you, and it builds their confidence." I remembered how my Dad had always had me watch him repair his cars or had me hold the light so I could learn how to analyze things and build what he always called "a working knowledge."

So, I thought, *Well, let's see what Kennedy can do, even if it costs me extra time.* I started by asking him if he thought he could figure out how to remove the frame from the wall. I was blown away when he started leaning inside the vent looking for screws that would hold the frame in the wall. He would look on one side, make a *hmmm* noise, then look on the other side. After a few minutes, I asked, "Do you want Daddy to show you where the screws are?"

He said, "No, Daddy. I am going to fix it." So, he hunted for the screws a while longer, and when I least expected it, he spotted the screws that were hidden behind the edge of the frame. In amazement, and with a great deal of excitement, I watched my four-year-old son remove all six of the screws that held the vent frame in the wall. After he had removed all the screws, he actually started pulling on the frame to remove it from the wall. I was thinking, *Dang, Bob the Builder is doing a better job than I ever realized teaching Kennedy how things work.*

After Kennedy removed the frame from the wall, I helped him put the new frame in place, and he decided I could put all the screws back so he could go work on his workbench instead. To this day, I couldn't tell you how much extra time it took to change out the vent that day, but I can tell you that that time together made for a memory I will never forget—and maybe one that he won't forget, either.

I had influence over Kennedy that day: I could show him love by sacrificing my time and letting him help me change out the vent, modeling an example of how we all should live, or I could follow my own desires and influence him to value his own needs first. I am learning that the most powerful way to impact other people's lives and add value to your own life is to sacrifice your time for others, and that is never truer than with your own family. I can live selfishly fearful and overly protective of my time, or I can live fearlessly generous about sharing my time with others. I only have so much time to live, so much time to give. Making that time count ought to be a primary goal, not hoarding it all for myself.

Love is generously sharing your time. Fear steals your time. Love generates fruit, abundance; fear starves and kills relationships. Love belongs in this story, in this memory. Fear has no place here. And love bears fruit, sometimes beyond what we ourselves can see through the influence we have on others.

CHAPTER THIRTEEN

Little Blue House

My oldest daughter, Faith, has now become a teenager. I can hardly believe it! Faith is truly beautiful inside and out, just like her mother. Faith is a very considerate and respectful young lady. She stands out among other young people her age. From my school days, I remember how easy it is for young people to be unkind to their peers. So, I am always trying to find ways to help my children make a conscious effort to value others in love.

I remember that when I was in elementary school, junior high school, and the first years of high school, I had a lot of friends—until all the kids in my age group grew taller and I didn't. That's when I went from my classmates scrambling to save me a chair at lunch tables to spending my lunch breaks eating by myself. For two years, no one wanted to sit with me because I was shorter than my classmates, and it didn't do anyone's reputation any good to be sitting with me.

During those years, I learned things I had never considered before. People I had inadvertently ignored before now became my friends. I learned firsthand what it was like to be overlooked. I also learned that everyone in school had fears. They just had different degrees of different fears. The funny thing was that most of us thought we were the only ones who were afraid. By the time I was a senior in high school, I had gained some height and attention as an aspiring water ski jumper and had been welcomed back to the lunch tables I had once sat at. But those tables didn't interest me anymore. It wasn't that I didn't like my former friends anymore but that I had developed a new perspective that helped me see more than just myself and what made me feel comfortable or uncomfortable.

One day, I was talking about all this to Faith, Grace, Kennedy, and their friend, Kacie, from across the street. As we sat on our front porch, I was trying to help them understand the importance of valuing others. About that time, an ambulance came streaking down the street. It passed right in front of our house and turned into a driveway about three houses down. That driveway led to a little blue house that was hidden by a few trees and sat a few hundred feet off the road. The kids claimed they had never seen the little blue house. I was kind of shocked since they all had lived in this neighborhood since birth.

Then it hit me that this little blue house posed the perfect example to help them see how important it is to be aware of others. I explained to them that the house had been there for years, and I started asking what became a series of questions, beginning with this one: "How do you think it makes the little blue house feel knowing you pass by it every day and never noticed it? How would you feel if you were the little blue house?"

They replied that the little blue house was probably sad.

I asked them, "Do you think the little blue house thinks you like it or don't like it?"

They replied that maybe the little blue house thought they didn't like it.

So, I asked them, "Since you see the blue house now, what do you think about it?"

They all said they really liked it and thought it was pretty.

I asked, "Do you think the little blue house knows that?"

"I guess not," they all answered.

"How do you think it would make the little blue house feel if you just waved when you passed by or maybe just told it one time you thought it was pretty and you liked it?"

It would probably make the little blue house feel really good, they responded.

I explained to them that, in life, we all are like the little blue house sometimes. We all feel little and left out at times—maybe in big ways or maybe in small ways, but no one ever gets through this life without at some point feeling left out or left behind or forgotten. Sometimes it's at school, sometimes at work, sometimes in a new neighborhood or town, sometimes even in our own homes, but the feeling that others don't care or don't value us will most certainly come.

What matters most in these times is not how we are feeling but what we believe. Do we also believe we are worthless? Or do we know better and believe the truth that none of us are worthless? If we value the little houses in our lives, then we will value ourselves when we live in them, and we will value the truth. If we don't value the truth, then we will value ourselves less than we valued the little blue houses that never truly lacked any value at all. "We think what we think and we do what we do because we believe what we believe," my friend Pastor Ron Hammonds always says.

That day on the porch, I talked to Faith, Grace, Kacie, and Kennedy about the difference we can make in others' lives by simply going a little out of our way or by being aware of others instead of living trapped in our own minds. I explained how I pray every day that my children will always understand their own value, no matter what life brings their way.

I told them that if we don't each go a little out of our way to value the people living in those little blue houses around us, one day we may not value ourselves, because one day we will be living in one of those little blue houses—all of us have days and seasons where we are overlooked.

You see, the truth can be found anywhere, at any time, with anyone, of any color, size, shape, or race—and a courageous person is always ready to hear it from anyone at any time. It doesn't matter if someone is the president of the United States or the guy stumbling through a parking lot with all his belongings in a plastic sack. If we don't value all people, then we are holding up a measuring stick or a standard that becomes, for us, the hurdle to a person's value. If a person clears this hurdle, then we give that person value; and if that person can't clear this hurdle, then we don't give that individual any value. Whatever hurdle we establish for others to clear forms a base we set as the standard for which we value our own lives. But for us to value ourselves, then, we must clear a hurdle even higher. You see, fear will lead us to set a standard to value others, and then we will judge ourselves even tougher than that standard we set for others.

We all find ourselves falling short from time to time. It's critically important that we know and value the truth that every person has equal value regardless of their current circumstances. Performance and finances and social status don't determine anyone's worth. The truth holds the same value in the White House as it does in the little blue house. If we value the little blue house, then when the day comes when we live in that little blue house, we will still value ourselves.

CHAPTER FOURTEEN

When Love Means Walking Away

In some cases, one person can love and love and love and never receive love, because the other person won't or can't find the courage to love back. At some point, in those cases, the most loving thing the loving person can do is walk away for the sake of the selfish person. I don't think the loving person should ever stop choosing to love. If a person will forever persist in selfishness, at some point a loving person becomes selfish by not being willing to suffer the heartbreak or uncertainty of separation, even though the loving person is enabling the selfish person to live a fruitless life.

If someone is physically harming you or anyone in your family, get out. Get away. That relationship must be ended immediately until it is completely apparent the relationship is safe to resume—if ever. If someone will physically harm you, then you should get out of the relationship to stay safe. Protecting yourself and your loved ones is not only best for you, it's also best for the abuser. Report the abuse. Get whatever professional help is appropriate, and listen to and heed what those professionals advise. In most cases, if someone is physically hurting us, love demands we refuse to allow them to continue to destroy themselves through the abuse they are showing. We cannot allow them to ignore the truth of what they are doing. Walking away is the only loving choice we can make.

You see, in any relationship, be it with a spouse, parent, sibling, friend, or neighbor, if one person is courageous and loving, then love will rule his or her life. If the other person is afraid and selfish, then fear will rule that person's life, even though the other person is showing love.

As you look at these trees, you can see that love does not rule our lives when we are loved. Love rules our lives when we love. But sometimes, after we have exhausted all other efforts, if a person persists in selfishness, we must love them enough to walk away. If we don't walk away, the other person will never grow or change, and we have enabled the other person to live a fruitless and fearful life—something love would never do.

I read once in a prominent author's book that he had noticed, in preaching funerals, a strange and unexpected reaction. He said he found that in relationships where an abusive spouse survived the death of their abused spouse, the abuser would show extreme grief, to the point of climbing into the coffin with their lost spouse. He attributed this reaction to guilt for having abused the person who was now deceased. I also found that reaction strange, since you would think the abusive person would perhaps show less grief, not more. After much thought about love and how it works, I feel I understand this seeming contradiction better. Though abusers may feel guilt at the funeral of their abused spouse, I don't think guilt is what results in the extreme grief. I think abusers know, somewhere inside themselves, that they were living off the fruit of the person they abused, and without them, they are now completely bankrupt.

Look at the trees. If one spouse is abusive toward a person who actually loves him or her, then the fruitless tree is not the abused; it is the abuser. The loving person will be producing fruit whether or not that fruit is taken by their abuser. (By the way, let me state again that if someone is abusing you, then you are loving no one by allowing it.)

Now imagine that the abusive person dies. The loving, but abused, person has lost someone he or she loved, so the abused person certainly grieves. But that grief is sustained by the love that mostly rules his or her life. In other words, the abused person has lost a lot, but not everything.

But if the abused person dies, then the abusive person has lost everything. He or she was living off the fruit or love in the life of the person who died, and the abusive partner is personally fruitless and rootless. They have nothing.

I believe that in funerals such as that author described, this is why abusive partners show signs of extreme grief at the deaths of their spouses. While a loving person may experience extreme grief, there is a difference between hopeless grief and grief sustained by love. Looking at this circumstance outside in, it makes no sense why someone who abused someone would have any grief, since the abusive partner didn't care enough about their partner not to abuse them. But when we look at the relationships and loss from the inside out, it all makes perfect sense.

Fear sees life outside in, and love sees life inside out. Without knowing anything about anyone, you can know why a relationship is unhealthy. It's because the eight things that love is not (or, you could say, the eight things that fear is) are ruling the hearts, and ultimately the actions, of one or both people. On the other hand, without knowing anything about anyone, you can know why a relationship is healthy: because the seven things of love are ruling the relationship. In both cases—living the eight things love is not or the seven things that love is—that choice is ours and within our control.

Allowing abuse is one of those choices. If you or someone you know is being abused, or if you know someone who continuously manipulates and takes advantage of you, living off your fruit and savaging their own roots again and again, walk away in love. Don't let them do this through you. Better they learn the truth of what they are doing now, when they have their best chance to change, than later, when that decision is no longer in their hands.

CHAPTER FIFTEEN

Unexpected Blessings of Love

The first shall be last, and the last shall be first. We have discussed this concept and others extensively throughout this book. What you do does not matter so much as why you do it—whether your actions stem from a loving desire to put God and the people around you before yourself or from a fearful distrust that love will protect you and a selfish desire to win first. Focusing on the fruit or the blessings in your life will cut you off from the source that produces them, and putting others before yourself, seeking the truth for the sake of others, and fighting to live a loving life does not always result in immediate blessings. Striving to live a loving life will result in the only true blessings life has to offer, but the crazy part—or maybe the sanest part—is that giving must be done with a pure heart, not with ulterior motives. But when it is, the blessings we do receive are sweeter for the way they surprise us and more genuine for the purity that produced them.

I fail miserably most of the time in my efforts to live a loving life, but I keep trying, and sometimes, the results that come to me out of the love others return to me are the most memorable gifts of my life.

In 2004, I was training for the 2004 Water Ski National Championships. I had won the 1996 National Championship and the bronze medal in 2003 and was looking forward to a great season. It was early in the season, and my second jump of the summer changed my hopes from praying I could win another national championship to praying I could walk and run with my kids again. I landed a jump with my left ski pointed sideways because of a mistake I made on the ramp. The resulting injury left me with a dislocated knee and worse. I completely tore three of my four ligaments and partially tore my only remaining ligament. It was the worst injury of my career.

My doctors, Michael McMahon and Jack Johnston, referred me to a physician in Houston, Texas, by the name of Walter Lowe. Dr. Lowe was the chief orthopedic surgeon for the University of Texas Medical Center and chief orthopedic physician for the Houston Texans NFL football team. His wife, Dawn Lowe, was his surgical assistant.

I met with them hoping they could help me recover well enough to walk and run again, maybe even ski jump again. Long story short, Dr. Lowe and Dawn gave me back the use of my leg by performing surgery and reconstructing a knee that was damaged nearly beyond repair. If Dr. Lowe and Dawn hadn't sacrificed most of their lives to become the best at what they do, I could have been crippled for life. I saw the dozens of patients pouring in and out of their clinic, imagined the workload, witnessed the two of them and their staff still going strong every time I left their office at 6 p.m. after an appointment, and realized I owed them more than payment. I owed them a sincere thank-you.

So, I emailed them and told them I was aware of the sacrifices they made in order to help people. I thanked them for reconstructing my knee and wrote that I would be forever grateful. Lest they forget or discount the fruit of their sacrifice, I wanted them to know what their daily service and commitment had meant to me and my family.

In the years following, my family and I somehow became what their staff called Dr. and Dawn Lowe's favorite patients. None of that made sense to me and my family. I had only wanted to express our incredible gratefulness for their gift to us of restoring my knee.

Sometime later, my son had a health scare, and Dr. Lowe made sure Kennedy was cared for immediately. Then, when my father fell ill, Dr. Lowe sent my dad to the best physician in Houston, who quickly diagnosed my father's condition and treated him. My dad saw a full recovery as a result. I had not shared my gratitude with Dr. Lowe and Dawn to receive anything—only to thank them for what they had done for me and my family. But it turned out that the Lowes were such loving people that loving them just resulted in further blessings for me.

Barbecue with a Dash of Love

I'll share another example. I have a favorite barbecue restaurant called Patillo's. It's been around for generations. The cook is a young man who stays in the back all day working hard to prepare meals for customers. He isn't really outgoing, but he makes the best dang brisket or smoked ham sandwich in the country. I could see he rarely got a thank-you. He never had when I was there (and I can go there as many as three times a week).

One day, I decided to ask his name and to thank him for the amazing sandwiches. I kept trying to make eye contact with him but never could. After a few more trips to the restaurant, I just walked around the register and got his attention to introduce myself and thank him. My only goal was to encourage him. He told me his name was Alvin. He didn't seem too impressed with my words of encouragement. I took off my stainless steel Shield of Strength weight-plate necklace with Philippians 4:13 inscribed on it, and I gave it to him. He didn't seem too impressed with that either.

Each time I returned to the restaurant for another sandwich, I would say hello to Alvin, and each time, his smile got just a little bigger, and so did my brisket sandwiches. Now, I also have to say, "Hey, Alvin, can I get a little bread with all that meat?" If I had complained the few times my sandwich had been thin on meat or maybe too fatty, never considering why or what it would cost Alvin, things at that restaurant might be very different. But when I put Alvin first, I found I was put first, because Alvin is a loving man.

All I am trying to say is that we create our own world as we live either from love or fear. In time, all our relationships are built either for others or for ourselves. When they are built for others, the blessings seem to keep coming for us; and when the relationships are built for ourselves, we have to fight for everything we want.

In time, as you live a loving life building loving relationships everywhere you go, you find yourself so surrounded by love that all you feel is grateful and undeserving. I also have a few stories about times I showed love to people who never loved in return, but not many. Almost everyone has the courage to love when they are loved. The question is who among us will love when they are not loved, because for them love will rule their lives no matter what.

I believe we are called to encourage each other, especially when we see others living out love, disregarding how much it might be costing them. When we live consumed in fear over what we might lose, we can't always see the love being poured out for us. But when we cast away our fears and focus on the seven things love is, we can more likely see and receive the abundance of love being sent our way as we begin to give some of that love back, so long as we always remember to love for love's sake—because of the love that has been shown to us. When love rules our lives, the fruit of that love is more than we can ever manipulate from others even if we tried.

140

CHAPTER SIXTEEN

From the Heart

Throughout this book, I have tried to clearly show that the decisions we make and the actions we take form the roots of our lives. These decisions and actions are based either on the seven things love is or on the eight things love is not. The fruit of these actions and decisions produces a life of fruitfulness or fruitlessness. While these statements are true, they are not the whole truth.

In truth, patience, kindness, truth, protectiveness, trust, hope, and perseverance are also fruit. They are the fruit of the things stored up in our hearts. We make decisions and take actions based on what we have already lived out in our minds and hearts. It's not possible to spend time in my mind and heart defending myself without regard for God and others and then, in life, to act on the seven things that love is. What rules my heart will rule my actions and decisions and, ultimately, will determine whether love or fear will rule my life.

I'll again quote my friend Ron Hammonds, who often says, "We think what we think, feel what we feel, and want what we want because we believe what we believe." I don't believe it's possible to choose to be the seven things love is and resist the eight things love is not simply through the power of the mind. Emotions and feelings are too powerful, and they persevere for a lifetime. In other words, fighting our emotions and feelings is a never-ending battle fighting our own wills to save ourselves—a battle in which the enemy never tires.

In order for the roots in our lives to be loving, we must first have a heart filled with love. The roots draw their nourishment from the soil around them. The decisions we make and the actions we take flow naturally out of the heart. When I say heart, I don't mean your blood pumper or brain. I mean the spirit—the innermost parts of your being. From the heart, the mouth speaks.

There is a big difference between your heart and your feelings. When someone offends you and you have a good heart, you may have feelings that tempt you to cut off your own roots from love, but if you stop to see the situation inside out, and if you consider love, then the feelings begin to mean nothing, because the heart is overriding the feelings. The heart is far more powerful than feelings. But if your heart is full of the eight things love is not, then when someone offends you, even if you find the strength to set the feelings aside and look within your own heart, what you will find is the eight things love is not. In that case, there is no power in man or woman able to overcome the drive to cut off our own roots.

If the heart is bad, then bad roots become the fruit of the heart, and the fruit of bad roots is a fearful, selfish, lonely, and hurting life of fruitlessness. On the other hand, if the heart is good, then the fruit of a good heart is healthy roots: a fruitful, courageous, and love-ruled life.

When people say that until you first love yourself, you can't love anyone else, I think what they mean is that until love rules your life, you can't love anyone else. What is misleading about the way that wisdom is often phrased is that it tells us to put ourselves first when the truth is that until you set yourself aside and love the God who first loved you, love will likely never rule your life.

A CHANGE OF HEART

How do we change our hearts so they can be ruled by love instead of fear?

Before we discuss this, let me give one more example for clarity. Look at the house, building, or car you're in. Before that structure ever existed, it first had to exist on paper. Before it existed on paper, it had to exist in someone's mind. It would be impossible for that structure to exist before someone first spent hours, days, and weeks envisioning the structure.

Then the fruit of that internal effort was drawn on paper, if someone had the courage to risk failing. After that, the fruit of what was on the paper became the structure, if someone had the courage to risk losing something. The only other option would be to randomly start nailing things together and see what happened.

For the person doing the thinking, drawing, and planning, the building progress seems slow to nonexistent until the actual construction begins. Then, in no time, the structure is complete and sturdy because the foundation was built carefully according to an intentional plan. In other words, someone took care of the roots—planning carefully, building on a foundation—and the fruit took care of itself. The building is the fruit in this example.

For the person who just randomly starts nailing things together without a plan, the progress seems immediate and can seem exciting for a while. However, in a short while, it becomes evident that things aren't fitting properly, and the only way to solve the problem is to tear everything down and start over. That is even harder to do once you are halfway through the construction. It was exciting to start, but you ignored what you knew was wrong.

Sometimes we build our lives the same way. We just begin living in the way that seems best to us. Before long, we find ourselves trapped, and we try to find an immediate solution. We keep patching and cutting corners until we end up living out a lifelong battle of trying to build and maintain what should have been the fruit of our efforts. It takes humility and surrender to admit we began living in the wrong way and to ask for help. There are only two choices, though. We either find the courage to surrender and change, or we live a life fighting a futile battle with ourselves and others for our fruit. To that end, we discover that we can only live off the fruit of others, because we have rendered ourselves fruitless.

If we think, dream, and live the eight things that love is not, then we will never construct a fruitful tree. We end up hanging fake fruit, boasting of our skills in hopes no one will notice our fruitlessness. When no one is looking, we are hopeless. On the other hand, if we think, dream, and live the seven things love is, then when we are tempted to cut off our own roots, we will find the courage to set ourselves aside and look inside our own hearts. That is the blueprint or plan that will set us right. What is in the heart will empower us to make decisions and take actions that will keep our own roots connected and will direct us to a fruitful life ruled by love.

Here is the last and final problem. After one's heart has been broken, either by people, life, circumstances, or fear, the heart can't really be healed unless it is guided by the seven things love is. In other words, the people who hurt us can't heal us, and we can't heal ourselves. Only loving can and will heal a heart. Being loved helps, but it is not required. What is required is loving. The only way for love to rule our hearts is to accept love into our hearts and let love fill our hearts. The Bible says God is love, and the truths laid out in this book help support that.

Jesus was the perfect example of love. He gave everything, expecting nothing in return, and paid a price for our sins, hoping only that others would love Him back. Jesus said that everything in heaven and on earth is fulfilled in love. He said that there are ten commandments but that one fulfills them all: to love the Lord your God with all your heart, mind, and soul, and to love your neighbor as yourself.

Jesus's example shows how we should set ourselves aside for others and God. If we do that, our lives will be ruled by love and will have the best chance to be fruitful. Jesus also said that in the Kingdom of God, the person who puts himself first will find himself last, and the person who puts himself last will find himself first. We could say that he who puts himself first will find himself fruitless, and he who puts himself last will find himself fruitful. If you know anyone who always puts himself before others, where do others put that person?

Jesus also said if someone slaps you on one cheek, turn the other. I used to think this was a bad interpretation, but when you realize that you only have two choices—one, to risk getting hurt a little more, and the other, to cut off your own roots—it makes perfect sense to turn the other cheek. But it takes great courage. Consider again that day on Calvary, when people were mocking Jesus while He hung on a cross for doing nothing wrong. He prayed, "Forgive them, for they know not what they do." When one of the two men hanging on a cross near Him mocked Jesus, Jesus didn't even respond. In response to the first criminal's mockery, however, the second criminal said, "we are punished justly, for we are getting what our deeds deserve. But this man has done nothing wrong." In love, he recognized Christ's innocence and asked Jesus to remember him. Jesus responded by saying the man would be with Him in paradise.

Why do you think Jesus told a man who had committed a selfish crime and was being crucified that he would be in heaven? I believe it is because the very moment before, the man had surrendered his heart and humbled himself. The man realized that Jesus, the innocent man being mocked on the cross, really was the Son of God. The moment this common man loved the Son of God (putting Jesus before himself), the love of God filled the man's heart. Connected to the love of God, in that moment, the roots of this man became the seven things love is, which allowed him to speak out of his heart. Love ruled his life in a moment, and the Son of God told him he would be in heaven.

This man did not have the opportunity to fulfill one religious requirement. He only had the opportunity to love God. That is all it takes. Loving God is all that is needed to change the heart. Loving God changes us from the inside out, and we are born again out of that love. Our old, selfish hearts are immediately filled with love; our roots stem out of their connection to healthy soil, the fruit of that love, and produce the fruit of love in our lives, no matter what the situation. If you're reading this book and you know that the love of God isn't feeding your decisions to try to live a loving life, I encourage you to go to God's Word, pray about all this, examine your own heart, and seek the truth. If I am right and these thoughts are the truth, then I believe the only logical conclusion is that Jesus Christ is your Savior and mine. Accept Him, love Him as much as you can, read His Word, and watch your heart slowly fill with a love that pushes fear away. You don't have to defeat fear in your life. Love will defeat it for you if you have the courage to set your self-concern aside and live out God's truth from the heart.

Chapter Seventeen

A Legacy of Love

I will close this book with this true story, which I hope makes sense to you and brings all these thoughts on love and fear together. This true story is about my grandfather, Ed Vaughan. He was a giving and unselfish man. I am told he stood about five feet seven inches tall. He was of medium build. He had dark hair and blue eyes—a fit-looking and handsome man. The "uniform" he always wore was overalls and suspenders. He was much like most great men—simple, hardworking, loving, and selfless. His faith was very important to him, my family tells me. He was a member of the local church and repaired cars in his spare time so he could afford to send my dad and his brother to a Christian school.

Growing up, I always felt my greatest loss was never knowing my grandfather. I still feel that way today. His love and the example of love he lived out would have surely enriched my life even more than the stories I've heard about him. My aunts and uncles often told my siblings and me the story of how Grandpa once pulled a family from a burning car that had flipped in a ditch.

He was the bravest man I can ever imagine, but also the most loving. They say he was always helping other people. Until writing this book, his influence in my life was mostly the knowledge that I was the son of a strong and loving family. I think a lot of my father and have never known anyone who thought more of their father than my father thought of his.

My grandfather worked at Magnolia Oil Company in Beaumont, which eventually, through a series of buyouts and consolidations, became part of what we know today as ExxonMobile. But back when it was still only Magnolia Oil Company, my grandfather was so good at what he did for them that when he was drafted, management appealed to the government to cancel his deployment because he was a leader in the manufacturing of airplane fuel used by the military.

Though my grandfather felt torn about how he could best serve his country and wanted to fight for his country, the military supported Magnolia Oil Company's suggestion and withdrew his draft papers so my grandfather could continue to lead a civilian team producing the fuel.

Ed enjoyed skating and fishing. My grandmother said he could stand on the beach for hours with a rod in his hand, sometimes from dawn until dusk, waiting on one bite. Since skates were hard to come by, he would take high-top tennis shoes and attach wheels to them so he and his daughter, Bertha, could skate together on the street near their home and at the local roller-skating rink.

In the years following the war, he purchased a few books and taught himself how to repair his own vehicles to save his family money and keep his vehicles on the road in good running order. He built his own shop behind his home to work on cars. Before long, he was repairing his friends' cars to help them stay on the road in a day when cars and mechanics were few and far between.

Ed was a perfectionist. As a mechanic, he would always take time to clean every engine and car part he touched, and he always sanded and repainted any part he repaired. As a result, all you had to do was open the hood of your repaired car and have a quick look to see where he had been working, because that place would be the cleanest and prettiest place under the hood.

This was also true in his life. If Ed had been anywhere or with anyone, you knew it. He always left things better than he found them and people better than before he had spent time with them. Through the years he worked at the Magnolia Oil Company, Ed's superiors came to understand that anyone who worked with Ed would become a better and more productive worker. His influence was that positive and that powerful. In the last few years he worked for the company, any time Magnolia management had someone they felt needed to be fired due to poor work or lack of responsibility, instead of letting them go, they would send them to work under Ed. A few months with Ed Vaughan, and they were the best hands in the plant—not because he was a tough boss but because he was a great leader.

Ed was humble enough to put others before himself. He cared so much that he told them the truth. He did this to help them improve, and because he did it with love, people knew Ed was not trying to manipulate them. His selfless and sincere heart opened for all to see. Combined with his tough work ethic, Ed had the kind of leadership anyone was willing to follow. If you knew Ed, you knew he was well educated in what he did. You could trust his knowledge. More important, you knew he would put you before the mission and himself.

By 1956, my grandfather had spent the previous twenty years working for Magnolia Oil as the company's leading expert in the manufacturing of airplane fuel. But in November, he went to his supervisor with the news that he had decided to leave Magnolia Oil Company and go work full time for himself as a mechanic. His supervisor asked him to stay another six months, and my grandfather agreed.

Just after midnight, on Easter Sunday, April 21, 1957, Ed would find himself in a place no one could ever imagine. He would be trying to find his way out of an explosion through a massive firestorm, when staying alive and just breathing must have seemed impossible. He had almost completed those last six months preceding his retirement from Magnolia Oil Company. In those months, he had picked up some maintenance contracts for the local milk and paper delivery trucks to begin the new phase in his life of service to others.

On Easter Eve, Ed headed into work for the night shift, knowing the clock was counting down his last days with Magnolia Oil and anticipating the future. There was a young man Ed had been working with, and in the bigger picture of things, I know my grandfather was really helping that young man. The young man, T. B. Hensley, had grown close to Ed.

That night, Ed and T. B. had begun working on some notoriously dangerous equipment in the plant when Ed heard a hissing sound. Ed knew this hissing sound meant the unit was beyond saving and that he and T. B. better run for their lives. He screamed, "Run, T. B.! Run!"

At 12:55 a.m. on Easter Sunday, before the two men were able to get clear of the unit, it exploded like a bomb. It was reportedly one of the worst explosions in Magnolia Oil's history. Fire engulfed the refinery in a time when firefighting gear was limited to a large water hose. The heat was so intense that no rescue workers could get anywhere near the fire, so they were forced to stand at a distance, attempting to reach the fire with their high-pressure water hoses. As they sprayed their water onto the fire, an ambulance stood by in the unlikely event anyone had survived the explosion. As time passed, everyone began to accept that no one could have survived that heat for that long.

But about that time, my grandfather came stumbling out of the fire. His frame appeared as a shadowed silhouette against the fire, and his body was completely engulfed in flames. Most of his clothes had been burned off, and his skin was as black as coal. Many of his features had been burned away, including his ears, nose, lips, and fingers. His skin was literally melting off his body. Rescue medics extinguished the flames that were burning his body. As they attended to him, the medics could not help but ask him how he had been able to walk out of the fire. They were looking at a man with second- and third-degree burns over 100 percent of his body.

Ed talked to them and told them why he'd come walking out of that fire. "I knew I was going to die, but I wanted to tell my family goodbye. Please, someone help me find T. B."

But no one ever saw T. B. again. I am told that in the days after the fire finally burned down, the remnants of T. B.'s boots were discovered in the ashes.

An ambulance transported my grandfather to the local hospital while authorities began to notify the families. Most of our family members were in town, but Ed's oldest son, Robert Vaughan (my father), was on his way to California. Robert had stopped in Houston to spend the night before continuing his trip to California, and family members managed to locate him. They called with the news of his father's serious injuries.

My father jumped in his car and started back down the road he had come, driving as fast as he could to reach his father. He arrived at the hospital six hours after the explosion. Upon entering the hospital, he walked past the room of a man clearly suffering and moaning in agony—not realizing that man was his own father, burned far beyond recognition.

The nurses directed my dad back to his father's room. As soon as my grandpa saw his son, he forced himself to rise above his pain, stopped his moaning, dried his tears, and said, "Bobby, I am OK, and everything is going to be all right. I have made my peace with God."

Ed told his oldest son that he knew he was going to die soon and asked my father to take care of the family. Dad said Grandpa asked the doctors for water, but they said it would only make things worse. He asked if they could just put a piece of ice on his tongue, but the doctors refused, because they felt even that would make things worse.

In the short time remaining in my grandfather's life, he made sure he told each of his children and his wife that he loved them and said his goodbyes to them. He died only seven hours after he walked out of that plant explosion in the dark hours before dawn on Easter Sunday.

In his dying words, he said to the family, "Meet me in heaven." Then he whispered to his wife, "Please don't forget to put the Easter baskets out for the kids."

That blows me away every time. Imagine a heart so focused on others that in its dying moment, all it could think about was the well-being of others. Imagine turning his love for his family into the will to walk out of that fire, to endure excruciating pain to bid goodbye to the ones he loved, and to be concerned about the kids getting their Easter baskets.

I always wondered how my grandfather walked out of a fire that melted the skin off of his body and the coins in his pocket together into a solid lump of metal. In coming to realize what love really is, I began to understand that it was his love for his friend, his family, and his God that kept him alive and got him out.

My grandfather's example has challenged me through the years to have the courage to strive to live a loving life no matter what. Many times in my life, when I have faced things I was not sure I could overcome, I was inspired by my grandfather's courage: to love no matter what it cost me and no matter whether I overcame or not. Love has always led me out. My grandfather's life, his love, and his act of courage, fighting his way out of that fire, helped me to understand that selfless love is definitely not for sissies, but—on the contrary—selfless love stands as the most courageous and powerful force on the earth and requires the most courageous hearts to live out.

Love is the single most important tool in finding your way out of your own fires in life. Love gave my grandfather the courage, strength, will, and ability to find his way out of that refinery fire long after it should have been humanly possible, when he knew he would die, his skin was falling off of his body, and there was nothing left to do but suffer and die. Love can give you the ability to find your way through your trials, although it may not be the kind of love you first think about.

Much of my life, I thought love was a feeling for another person. I suspect many people think the same thing. As we've learned, feelings are the fruit of love, not love itself. As a matter of fact, love in its purest state will set feelings completely aside.

Remember that love is an "undefeatable benevolence," an "unconquerable" goodwill that always seeks the highest good of others, no matter what they do. It gives freely without asking anything in return and does not consider the worth of its object. Love is a choice, not a chance; and it is a will, not an emotion.

Love is a decision, not a feeling. In all of life, there are two main motives behind every action and thought. Everything is either centered in the self or centered in others. Self will always look out for self, and love will always look out for others. It is easy to search for peace in this life and start looking out for yourself. The problem with looking out for yourself is that, in the end, all you have is yourself, and self was never meant to love self. We were meant to love others. When all we have is ourselves, we are empty and find little motivation to find or fight our way out of our trials. We feel hopeless.

Please don't misunderstand me. We need to be complete and secure, but if our security is found in ourselves, we will always be defending that security (or ourselves) so that we don't lose it. When we defend ourselves, we isolate ourselves and stop looking out for others. As counterintuitive as it may sound, everything we are looking for can be found when we learn to give it all away and put others first; and the only thing that can complete any of us is God's love living in us because we decided to love Him.

I like to say it like this: it is easy to spend your whole life chasing something that is impossible to catch, but if you will stop chasing and start helping others get what they need, then what you are looking for will chase you down. Not only will it chase you down, it will give you the power to walk out of your fire.

I'm not telling you to neglect yourself or to allow others to continually take advantage of you. Allowing others to take advantage of you is worse for them than it is for you anyway.

I don't think my grandfather would have found the strength to walk out of that fire for himself. I don't think fear would have brought him out of that fire, either. But for others, he had more than enough strength, courage, faith, and power to find his will and his way out.

For yourself, you may have a hard time finding your way out of whatever trials you encounter. For others, for love, and for your Lord, you can do more than you ever dreamed. Sometimes love gets us into things that only love can get us out of, but once we are in the fire, we too often abandon love to protect ourselves, not realizing that selfishness may ensure we never get out. Love got my grandfather out, and love will carry you out. We often fail to love, but love never fails.

You will find that fearful people will convince you they are strong. They know they are afraid, so they project strength. The more strength a fearful person projects, the more afraid he or she becomes, because such people have more to hide. Eventually, if they project enough strength and it seems to be working, they become dangerous. Outwardly, they become who they project, but on the inside, they are still afraid. So, whoever threatens to uncover who they really are will be subject to great persecution. For them, it would almost be easier to die than for other people to discover who they really are.

On the other hand, a truly strong and loving person will always project humility: not weakness, but true humility. These people also know they have a breaking point, but though they may be afraid, the love of God has given them the strength to persevere despite their own weakness and fears. They value the truth and others and have peace because they don't project what love can't support. We can all live a life ruled by love, but not until we have the courage to die to ourselves. The one thing that must come before a resurrection is death. The death of the old heart makes way for the truly loving heart to grow.

Remember my words earlier in this book: your life is not about you. It's way bigger and more important than that! Your life is about God and others.

I am forever thankful and forever changed because my grandfather had the courage to leave his family and those who knew him a legacy of love instead of a legacy of fear. I encourage you to do the same. Go and live a loving life! Get in the right fight—the fight for your roots, not your fruit! You can't do it for yourself, but it will be the best thing you ever did for yourself, I promise you. Trust God's word no matter what, and keep your eyes on the horizon.

John 15:5-10 King James Version (KJV)

I am the vine, ye are the branches: He that abideth in me, and I in him, the same bringeth forth much fruit: for without me ye can do nothing.

If a man abide not in me, he is cast forth as a branch, and is withered; and men gather them, and cast them into the fire, and they are burned.

If ye abide in me, and my words abide in you, ye shall ask what ye will, and it shall be done unto you.

Herein is my Father glorified, that ye bear much fruit; so shall ye be my disciples.

As the Father hath loved me, so have I loved you: continue ye in my love.

If ye keep my commandments, ye shall abide in my love; even as I have kept my Father's commandments, and abide in his love.

Scripture References

The following scripture references from the New International Version of the Holy Bible are helpful in understanding what God's word says about love and fear.

1 CORINTHIANS 13:1–8

"If I speak in the tongues of men and of angels, but have not love, I am only a resounding gong or a clanging cymbal. If I have the gift of prophecy and can fathom all mysteries and all knowledge, and if I have a faith that can move mountains, but have not love, I am nothing. If I give all I possess to the poor and surrender my body to the flames, but have not love, I gain nothing.

"Love is patient, love is kind. It does not envy, it does not boast, it is not proud. It is not rude, it is not self-seeking, it is not easily angered, it keeps no record of wrongs. Love does not delight in evil but rejoices with the truth. It always protects, always trusts, always hopes, always perseveres. Love never fails."

1 JOHN 4:19

"We love because he first loved us."

JOHN 3:16–17

"For God so loved the world that he gave his one and only Son, that whoever believes in him shall not perish but have eternal life. For God did not send his Son into the world to condemn the world, but to save the world through him."

DANIEL 3

The story of Shadrach, Meshach, Abednego, and King Nebuchadnezzar.

1 SAMUEL 17

The story of David and Goliath.

MATTHEW 26

The story of Judas's betrayal of Christ.

MATTHEW 12:34

"For out of the overflow of the heart the mouth speaks."

1 JOHN 4:7–8

"Dear friends, let us love one another, for love comes from God. Everyone who loves has been born of God and knows God. Whoever does not love does not know God, because God is love."

1 JOHN 2:2

"He is the atoning sacrifice for our sins, and not only for ours but also for the sins of the whole world."

MATTHEW 22:36–40

"'Teacher, which is the greatest commandment in the law?'

"Jesus replied: 'Love the Lord your God with all your heart and with all your soul and with all your mind.'

"This is the first and greatest commandment. And the second is like it: 'Love your neighbor as yourself.' . . . All the Law and the Prophets hang on these two commandments."

Matthew 19:30

"But many who are first will be last, and many who are last will be first."

Matthew 5:39

"If someone strikes you on the right cheek, turn to him the other also."

Luke 23:34

"Jesus said, 'Father, forgive them, for they do not know what they are doing.'"

Luke 23:39–43

"One of the criminals who hung there hurled insults at him: 'Aren't you the Christ? Save yourself and us!'

"But the other criminal rebuked him. 'Don't you fear God,' he said, 'since you are under the same sentence?'

"'We are punished justly, for we are getting what our deeds deserve. But this man has done nothing wrong.'

"Then he said, 'Jesus, remember me when you come into your kingdom.'

"Jesus answered him, 'I tell you the truth, today you will be with me in paradise.'"

Romans 10:9–10

"That if you confess with your mouth, 'Jesus is Lord,' and believe in your heart that God raised him from the dead, you will be saved. For it is with your heart that you believe and are justified, and it is with your mouth that you confess and are saved."

1 JOHN 5:11–13

"And this is the testimony: God has given us eternal life, and this life is in his Son. He who has the Son has life; he who does not have the Son of God does not have life.

"I write these things to you who believe in the name of the Son of God so that you may know that you have eternal life."

MATTHEW 7:15–20

"Watch out for false prophets. They come to you in sheep's clothing, but inwardly they are ferocious wolves. By their fruit you will recognize them. Do people pick grapes from thorn bushes, or figs from thistles? Likewise, every good tree bears good fruit, but a bad tree bears bad fruit. A good tree cannot bear bad fruit, and a bad tree cannot bear good fruit. Every tree that does not bear good fruit is cut down and thrown into the fire. Thus, by their fruit, you will recognize them."

JOHN 12:25

"Anyone who loves their life will lose it, while anyone who hates their life in this world will keep it for eternal life."

MATTHEW 18:21–22

"Then Peter came to Jesus and asked, 'Lord, how many times shall I forgive my brother or sister who sins against me? Up to seven times?' Jesus answered, 'I tell you, not seven times, but seventy times seven.'"

I JOHN 4:18

"There is no fear in love. But perfect love drives out fear, because fear has to do with punishment. The one who fears is not made perfect in love."

About the Author

Kenny Vaughan is a husband, a father of three, a world-class athlete, and a servant of Jesus Christ. Over the years, he has been featured in a number of interviews with national media, and his Instagram video posts (@johnkennedyvaughan) about love and faith inspire tens of thousands across the country.

Growing up, Kenny learned to water ski, to hunt and fish, to understand God's perfect love, and to honor God, country, and family. For fifteen years, he chased his dream of winning the national water ski long-jump championship, and, bolstered by the scriptures scrawled on his ski tow-rope handles, he achieved his dream against all odds. Vaughan took the scriptures that inspired him that day and had them inscribed on dog tags. He founded Shields of Strength, a company that distributes inspirational scripture engraved upon dog tags and other jewelry. The necklaces have become popular with professional and aspiring athletes—including Olympians, military personnel, law enforcement, students, and adults from all walks of life who find encouragement in scripture to face life's challenges.

Vaughan's first book, *Shields of Strength: One Man's Victory over Fear and What It Has Meant for America*, was published in 2010 by Brown Books. *The Right Fight: How to Live a Loving Life* turns its focus to fear's polar opposite: pure, unselfish love for others.

Kenny Vaughan lives in Southeast Texas, near Beaumont, with Tammie, the love of his life, and their three children.

To Learn More about the Vaughans and Their Ministry, Please Visit . . .
https://www.instagram.com/johnkennedyvaughan/
https://www.shieldsofstrength.com/
http://www.profnetconnect.com/kennyvaughan
https://point27.org/

For more information about
Shields of Strength
visit **shieldsofstrength.com**
or call 800-326-7882